WORDBUILD FOUNDATION

In *WordBuild Foundations Level 1*, you learned about compound words, prefixes and suffixes, and some special spelling rules with suffixes. The inside back cover of this book is a handy reference to many of the things that you learned.

Those spelling rules,
- doubling the final consonant with *–ed* and *–ing*
- dropping the final "e" with *–ed* and *–ing*

are a big part of what makes English, well, English!

Languages grow and change all the time. Have you ever wondered how a new word makes it into the dictionary? Who decides? You do! The very first prefix in this activity book is "dis", which is now a word all by itself in the dictionary. It made it into the dictionary because so many people used it and understood what it meant, as in "Don't *dis* Trudi's ideas about the costumes for the play!"

This year, you are going to learn quite a few new prefixes and suffixes. You are also going to use your knowledge of the spelling rules with some new suffixes. You will even learn another important spelling rule, *change y to i*. You will discover and build words with *two* suffixes. Near the end of the year, you will learn how some prefixes actually change their spelling depending on the word they are attached to.

The most important thing for you to learn is how words work. Once you know this, when you see a word you haven't seen before, you will ask yourself "*What do I already know about this word*?"

A person who can look at a new word and break it down into its meaningful parts is a:

| MORPHOLOGICAL PROBLEM SOLVER |

That is what YOU are about to become!

Copyright Dynamic Literacy LLC www.dynamicliteracy.com

PREFIX SQUARE

_____
Name

for **dis**- meaning "not, apart"

Start in the middle square with the prefix **dis** and combine this part with the words in the other squares to build new words. Write each word and a definition you can think of for it in the spaces provided at the bottom of the page. Use the back of the page if you need to.

honest	grace	please
obey	**dis-**	appear
trust	belief	charge

_____
_____
_____
_____
_____
_____

Copyright Dynamic Literacy LLC   www.dynamicliteracy.com

AFFIX ADDER

_____
Name

The prefix **dis**- means "not, apart"

1. Write **dis** in the blank space in front of each word listed below and make a new word.
2. Tell what you think the new word means.
3. Write a sentence using the new word.

We've done one for you:

APPROVE means to hold a favorable opinion of

...so DISAPPROVE means *to hold a not favorable opinion of.*

Sentence: *I disapprove of the decision to keep schools open year-round.*

___

1. AGREE means to hold the same opinion
   ...so ____ AGREE means _____

Used in a sentence:

2. APPEAR means to come into view
   ...so ____ APPEAR means _____

Used in a sentence:

3. ARM means to supply with a weapon
   ...so ____ ARM means _____

Used in a sentence:

4. CONTINUE means to go on with
   ...so ____ CONTINUE means _____

Used in a sentence:

Copyright Dynamic Literacy LLC   www.dynamicliteracy.com

5. **COURTEOUS** means polite
   ...so ____ COURTEOUS means _____
   Used in a sentence:

6. **GRACE** means to give pleasantness to
   ...so ____ GRACE means _____
   Used in a sentence:

7. **HONEST** means truthful
   ...so ____ HONEST means _____
   Used in a sentence:

8. **OBEY** means to follow orders
   ...so ____ OBEY means _____
   Used in a sentence:

9. **QUALIFY** means to declare fit to play
   ...so ____ QUALIFY means _____
   Used in a sentence:

10. **SIMILAR** means like another
    ...so ____ SIMILAR means _____
    Used in a sentence:

MAGIC SQUARE

_____
Name

for **dis**- meaning "not, apart"

Select the best definition for each of the words in the **dis** family. Put the number of the definition in the proper space in the Magic Square box. If the numbers going up and down and the numbers going across all add up to the same thing, you have found the magic number!

WORDS
- A. disabled
- B. displeased
- C. disobeying
- D. distrusting
- E. disassembled
- F. discourteous
- G. disappearance
- H. dissimilarity
- I. disagreeable

DEFINITIONS
1. not pleasant; likely to quarrel
2. taken apart; not put together
3. with power or ability taken away
4. feeling unable to rely on
5. not following orders or rules
6. quality of being unlike or different
7. not happy with
8. the act of passing out of sight
9. rude; with no manners

Magic Square Box

A.	B.	C.
D.	E.	F.
G.	H.	I.

Magic Number _____

Copyright Dynamic Literacy LLC   www.dynamicliteracy.com

Name _____

WORD SEARCH

Words with prefix dis- meaning "not, apart"

Find and circle all the words in the grid. Words can go across or up and down, straight or diagonally, forwards or backwards.

```
N J T Q T R O F M O C S I D D D D
W M J S J L Y R E V O C S I D Q I
M P D F U L Q S Q M Q V D S W X S
I E K I Y R O R L H X Y I H O B P
A C T Q S L T Z N L N R S O L D R
L J T A C P X S R Z E X B N L V O
C D N S C V L A I L G V E O A T V
S G I Q H O E A H D R R L R S V E
I D P S J P L M C T A X I K I P D
D H D P P Q N S M E H W E F D I D
K L I A X L X T I E C T V P S I R
D I S O R D E R S D S B E A S L L
R I F R Q B L A L K I H G A Y V P
D J A R T N E R S H D R R W Z K F
M K V X L S Z H K E E M M N P V L
M W O X I M D I S E M P O W E R N
M N R D N D I S A P P R O V E M J
```

disagree	disclaim	dishonor
disallow	disclose	dislocate
disappear	discomfort	disorder
disapprove	discovery	displace
disarm	disease	displease
disbelieve	disempower	disprove
discharge	disfavor	distrust

Name _____

Don't Dis Me

Fill in the blanks using the words below that all mean "not or opposite of".

Why do they mean <u>not or apart</u>? _____

1. Sue and I _____ about who the best singer is.

2. _____ people don't tell the truth.

3. Lazy people _____ when it is time to work.

4. Soldiers get in trouble if they decide to _____ orders.

5. You show _____ to your teacher by talking in class.

6. Some _____ people have to use a wheelchair.

7. The bad test results _____ my parents.

8. I had to _____ the power cord to move the TV.

9. Apple would _____ the iPod if people stopped buying them.

10. If I see people cheat, I feel _____ toward them.

<u>Check off these words as you use them.</u>

disabled	disappear	disconnect	disagree	displeased
distrust	disrespect	dishonest	discontinue	disobey

Copyright Dynamic Literacy LLC   www.dynamicliteracy.com

PREFIX/SUFFIX SQUARE

Name _____

for **dis-**, meaning "not, apart"
plus **-s** "he, she, or it does"

Start in the middle square with the prefix **dis** and the suffix **s** and combine both of these parts with the words in the other squares to build new words. Write each new word and the definition you can think of for it in the spaces provided at the bottom of the page. Use the back of the page if you need to.

believe	own	like
connect	dis- + -s	infect
figure	honor	locate

_____
_____
_____
_____
_____
_____

Copyright Dynamic Literacy LLC   www.dynamicliteracy.com

AFFIX ADDER

_____
Name

> The prefix **dis**- means "not, apart."
> The suffix **-s** means "he, she, or it does."
>
> 1. Write **dis** in the blank space before each word and **s** in the blank space after each word listed below and make a new word.
> 2. Tell what you think the new word means.
> 3. Write a sentence using the new word.

We've done one for you:

AGREE means to hold the same opinion

...so <u>DIS</u>AGREE<u>S</u> means <u>does not hold the same opinion.</u>

Sentence: My mother disagrees with my decision to become a vegetarian.

_____

1. APPROVE means to agree

   ...so ____ APPROVE ____ means _____

Used in a sentence:

_____

2. BELIEVE means to take as true

   ...so ____ BELIEVE ____ means _____

Used in a sentence:

_____

3. CONTINUE means to go on with

   ...so ____ CONTINUE ____ means _____

Used in a sentence:

_____

4. OBEY means to follow orders

   ...so ____ OBEY ____ means _____

Used in a sentence:

_____

Copyright Dynamic Literacy LLC   www.dynamicliteracy.com

5. PLACE means to put something
    ...so ____ PLACE ____ means _____
Used in a sentence:

6. ARM means to supply with a weapon
    ...so ____ ARM ____ means _____
Used in a sentence:

7. CONNECT means to join together
    ...so ____ CONNECT ____ means _____
Used in a sentence:

8. FAVOR means to show approval
    ...so ____ FAVOR ____ means _____
Used in a sentence:

9. INFECT means to cause to have germs
    ...so ____ INFECT ____ means _____
Used in a sentence:

10. ALLOW means to permit to happen
    ...so ____ ALLOW ____ means _____
Used in a sentence:

Copyright Dynamic Literacy LLC   www.dynamicliteracy.com

MAGIC SQUARE

Name _____

for **-dis** meaning "not, apart"
plus **-s** meaning "he, she, or it does"

Select the best definition for each of the words in the **dis** plus **s** families. Put the number of the definition in the proper space in the Magic Square box. If the numbers going up and down and the numbers going across all add up to the same thing, you have found the magic number!

WORDS
A. displeases
B. disconnects
C. disobeys
D. disregards
E. disrespects
F. disallows
G. disentangles
H. dislocates
I. disagrees

DEFINITIONS
1. causes to be out of place
2. does not bother about or look at
3. does not follow orders
4. does not permit
5. causes not to be joined together
6. causes not to be confused or mixed up
7. causes not to be happy
8. does not go along with
9. does not treat with honor or dignity

Magic Square Box

A. 7	B. 5	C. 3
D. 2	E. 9	F. 4
G. 6	H. 1	I. 8

Magic Number __15__

Copyright Dynamic Literacy LLC   www.dynamicliteracy.com

Name _____

WORD SEARCH

Words with the prefix dis- meaning "not, apart"
and the suffix -s, meaning "he, she, or it does"

Find and circle all the words in the grid. Words can go across or up and down, straight or diagonally, forwards or backwards

```
V P N K D I S A P P E A R S Q N S B
T J S T C E F N I S I D F R X E N N
B K H T F D T R W D H T V T C T H R
L R J N S L I O X T I K W A L S L W
G Y S L K T L S C T T S L J Y W D L
B G E C N L C H A C S P F E H I L S
N V U P A V D E Y P S E B A S L E R
D N N S H S I S N I P O K H V G R D
I L I T D E S E D N S R O I A O I W
S D T L I T A E H I O N O R L S R J
G K N P S A R R D R O C U V B S R S
R T O K F C M G P R Z O S E E K I K
A W C N I O S A S F C Q L I P S D D
C P S B G L V S D S X I D K D L J Z
E N I M U S F I I S E G D O L S I D
S N D M R I J D P V T R K G Y C Y M
V R F R E D I S E N T A N G L E S X
B T W Q S G W S M S R O L O C S I D
```

disagrees	disconnects	dishonors
disallows	discontinues	disinfects
disappears	discourages	dislikes
disapproves	disentangles	dislocates
disarms	disfavors	dislodges
disbelieves	disfigures	disobeys
discolors	disgraces	displaces

Name _____

Can't We All Just Get Along?

Fill in the blanks using the words below that all mean "he, she, or it does not or does the opposite of." Why do they mean <u>he, she, or it does not or does the opposite of</u>?
_____

1. When someone _____ the rules he or she can get in trouble.

2. Joachim _____ with Marta about the best way to walk to school.

3. Juanita _____ the taste of broccoli.

4. If the umpire _____ the goal, Ted's team will lose.

5. Spaghetti sauce _____ your shirt if you miss your mouth with the fork!

6. Mr. Johnson _____ Jim's story about the dog eating his homework.

7. Isn't it odd how everyone _____ when there is work to be done?

8. Juan _____ the power cord before taking the cover off his computer

9. I hate it when a company _____ a product I like.

10. A policeman _____ a criminal if he has a gun.

<u>Check off these words as you use them.</u>

disallows	dislikes	disappears	disobeys	discolors
discontinues	disconnects	disagrees	disarms	disbelieves

Copyright Dynamic Literacy LLC   www.dynamicliteracy.com

SUFFIX SQUARE

_____
Name

The suffix **-er** means "a person or device that does" whatever action is indicated by the word to which it is attached. When **–er** is attached to a one-syllable word ending in a consonant with a single vowel in front of it, the consonant is doubled.

Start in the middle square with the suffix **er** and combine this part with the words in the other squares to build new words. Remember to double the final consonant of the words to which you attach the suffix **er**. Write each word and a definition you can think of for it in the spaces provided at the bottom of the page. Use the back of the page if you need to.

shop	zip	rob
quit	-er	bat
plan	run	swim

_____
_____
_____
_____

Copyright Dynamic Literacy LLC   www.dynamicliteracy.com

AFFIX ADDER

_____
Name

> The suffix **-er** changes a verb into a word meaning "a person or device that does" whatever action is indicated by the verb. When **–er** is attached to a one-syllable word ending in a consonant with a single vowel in front of it, the consonant is doubled.
>
> 1. Write **er** in the blank space after each word listed below and make a new word. Remember to double the last letter
> 2. Tell what you think the new word means.
> 3. Write a sentence using the new word.

We've done one for you:
    SPIN means to turn around
    …so SPIN<u>NER</u> means <u>a device or person that turns around.</u>

<u>Sentence</u>: The spinner told us what move to make in the game.

_____

1. CHIP means to break into smaller pieces
   …so CHIP_____ means _____
<u>Used in a sentence</u>:

_____

2. CUT means to slice open with a sharp edged instrument
   …so CUT_____ means _____
<u>Used in a sentence</u>:

_____

3. HIT means to strike with force
   …so HIT_____ means _____
<u>Used in a sentence</u>:

_____

Copyright Dynamic Literacy LLC   www.dynamicliteracy.com

4. STIR means to mix or move around
   ...so STIR_____ means _____
Used in a sentence:

5. WRAP means to cover
   ...so WRAP_____ means _____
Used in a sentence:

6. SHIP means to send
   ...so SHIP_____ means _____
Used in a sentence:

7. TRAP means to catch or to ensnare
   ...so TRAP_____ means _____
Used in a sentence:

8. FIB means to tell an untruth
   ...so FIB_____ means _____
Used in a sentence:

9. TRIM means to decorate or cut back
   ...so TRIM_____ means _____
Used in a sentence:

10. GRAB means to take hold of suddenly
    ...so GRAB_____ means _____
Used in a sentence:

MAGIC SQUARE

_____
Name

The suffix **-er** can change a word to mean "a person or device that does" whatever action is indicated. When **-er** is attached to a one-syllable word ending in a consonant with a single vowel in front of it, the consonant is doubled.

Select the best definition for each of the words. Put the number of the definition in the proper space in the Magic Square box. If the numbers going up and down and the numbers going across all add up to the same thing, you have found the magic number!

WORDS
- A. flipper
- B. swapper
- C. scrubber
- D. digger
- E. clipper
- F. sitter
- G. stopper
- H. logger
- I. bidder

DEFINITIONS
1. one that hits up against suddenly
2. one who trades things
3. person who offers to buy, as at an auction
4. one who removes earth or other material
5. a device that prevents leaks
6. a trimming device
7. a person or device that rubs clean
8. one who cares for young children
9. a wide, flat part on sea animals used for swimming
10. a person who turns trees into lumber

Magic Square Box

A.	B.	C.
D.	E.	F.
G.	H.	I.

Magic Number _____

Copyright Dynamic Literacy LLC www.dynamicliteracy.com

Name _____

WORD SEARCH

Words with suffix -er, meaning "a person or device that does," with doubling.

Find and circle all the words in the grid. Words can go across or up and down, straight or diagonally, forwards or backwards.

```
S P O T T E R N P T H B J Q M
R E G G U L S T M Y R M X V L
E D T R E P P O H E W J P R D
P R S L L X H M P Y R L E C W
P O N T J N L P R T E G T K F
I P N J I P A E G E G D F K L
T P F V Z R P K K A G D F R I
H E S J W P R F B L U G A L P
R R T D I M M E R B L P U G P
E V O S B R V K R D P F R H E
P T P C R A E H G E I A T M R
P K P R Q Y T P R N B P Q L N
I L E G Q P N T P B W D P V Z
Z X R X L B P K E O L V Z E G
W P K I D D E R L R M M J B R
```

bagger	hopper	slugger
batter	hugger	spotter
dimmer	kidder	stirrer
dipper	mopper	stopper
dropper	plugger	tipper
flipper	rapper	wrapper
grabber	sipper	zipper

Name _____

Double Doer

Fill in the blanks using the words below that all mean "person or device that does."

Why do they mean person or device that does? _____

1. The _____ kept the beat for the marching band.

2. A calendar and _____ will help you organize better.

3. Howard and Jerry used a _____ to cut the grass away from the sidewalk.

4. Trixi is an ice cream _____ at the fair.

5. Paoli spilled a bucket of water, and a _____ came along to clean it up.

6. Every _____ in the store was looking for bargains.

7. The _____ at the swimming lessons learned fast.

8. Vinayak is such a _____ that no one can believe a word he says.

9. If you decide to be a _____, you'll never win any games.

Check off these words as you use them.

| bagger | dipper | fibber | planner | shopper |
| beginner | drummer | mopper | quitter | trimmer |

Copyright Dynamic Literacy LLC   www.dynamicliteracy.com

SUFFIX SQUARE

_____
Name

for -ed meaning "having been, or made to become"

Start in the middle square with the suffix -ed and combine this part with the words in the other squares to build new words. Write each word and a definition you can think of for it in the spaces provided at the bottom of the page. Use the back of the page if you need to.

salt	trust	darken
sunburn	-ed	frost
seat	slant	melt

_____
_____
_____
_____
_____
_____

Copyright Dynamic Literacy LLC   www.dynamicliteracy.com

AFFIX ADDER

Name _____

> The suffix **-ed** adjective means "having been, or made to become."

1. Write **ed** in the blank space after each word listed below and make a new word.
2. Tell what you think the new word means.
3. Write a sentence using the new word.

We've done one for you:

  GIFT means something special to give
  ...so GIFT<u>ED</u> means <u>having been given something special.</u>
<u>Sentence</u>: Danisha was gifted with a beautiful voice.

_____

1. SELECT means to choose
   ...so SELECT ____ means _____
<u>Used in a sentence</u>:

_____

2. SHORTEN means to make less long
   ...so SHORTEN ____ means _____
<u>Used in a sentence</u>:

_____

3. TOAST means to make brown with heat
   ...so TOAST ____ means _____
<u>Used in a sentence</u>:

_____

Copyright Dynamic Literacy LLC   www.dynamicliteracy.com

4. FROST means to coat with sugar
   ...so FROST ____ means _____
Used in a sentence:

5. SPIRIT means energy or liveliness
   ...so SPIRIT ____ means _____
Used in a sentence:

6. ASSIGN means to give a task to
   ...so ASSIGN ____ means _____
Used in a sentence:

7. ABANDON means to leave behind
   ...so ABANDON ____ means _____
Used in a sentence:

8. HELMET means protective headgear
   ...so HELMET ____ means _____
Used in a sentence:

9. CRACK means to break
   ...so CRACK ____ means _____
Used in a sentence:

10. OWN means to have as a possession
    ...so OWN ____ means _____
Used in a sentence:

MAGIC SQUARE

_____
Name

for -ed meaning "having been, or made to become"

Select the best definition for each of the words in the **ed** family. Put the number of the definition in the proper space in the Magic Square box. If the numbers going up and down and the numbers going across all add up to the same thing, you have found the magic number!

WORDS
- A. sharpened
- B. rented
- C. expected
- D. cracked
- E. tilted
- F. burned
- G. spirited
- H. selected
- I. filled

DEFINITIONS
1. having lots of trees
2. having been waited for; known to be coming
3. having been picked out
4. having been broken
5. having a lot of energy
6. hurt by fire
7. paid for to be used for a while; not owned
8. made to slant
9. made to have a point
10. completed up to the top
11. covered with a coat of color
12. cooked in a stew

Magic Square Box

A.	B.	C.
D.	E.	F.
G.	H.	I.

Magic Number _____

Copyright Dynamic Literacy LLC   www.dynamicliteracy.com

WORD SEARCH

Words with suffix -ed, meaning "having been, or made to become"

Find and circle all the words in the grid. Words can go across or up and down, straight or diagonally, forwards or backwards

```
Q J N C J R B N D Z F M Q Q C S
T R U S T E D Y E F L A W E D P
N R E N T E D M N K M D V Q X R
F Y T N Q V C D G Q F E P T Q A
T O T N N T E X I T R T D T N I
N L R Y S T F G S T O I E W K N
Y L X E S A I N S R S M N L D E
X C W A S F D U A E T I E E M D
M F O D T T N D L P E L T W E L
D T D E E B E E J D L E N T S
N M D E U T C D M N E P E Z R A
J J Q R T T E F W M E K W F C L
Q P N L E L Z M Y Y R D S N K T
K E K D M P I Y L A C R R L K E
D E T N U A H T D E Q B M H Z D
N X D E T I R I P S H Y V P B B
```

assigned	helmeted	spirited
darkened	limited	sprained
flawed	melted	sunburned
forested	rented	sweetened
frosted	saddened	tilted
gifted	salted	toasted
haunted	selected	trusted

MADE TO BE!

Fill in the blanks using the words below that all mean "having been, or made to become."

Why do they mean having been, or made to become?

_____

1. The trees around the volcano had been destroyed, but now after a few years the area is again _____.

2. For a _____ time, we can see the movie for free.

3. Aleeta didn't realize that her wrist was _____ until the pain started up later.

4. Molly rescued a little puppy that she found _____ along the road.

5. The heads of the _____ cyclers were not badly injured in the collision.

6. Danisha and Roy were _____ to learn the bad news.

7. Ramona was Tania's dearest and most _____ friend.

8. Everyone felt much better and their spirits were _____ to learn that Chantal and Marika were safe.

9. The stale-smelling room was _____ after we opened the windows and brought in some flowers.

10. Craig and Willa cannot stand slimy _____ tomatoes.

Check off these words as you use them.

abandoned	gladdened	limited	saddened	stewed
forested	helmeted	refreshened	sprained	trusted

PREFIX/SUFFIX SQUARE _____
Name

for **un**- meaning "not, opposite of, or absence of"
plus **-ed**, meaning "having been, or made to become"

Start in the middle square with the prefix **un** and the suffix **ed** and combine both of these parts with the words in the other squares to build new words. Write each new word and the definition you can think of for it in the spaces provided at the bottom of the page. Use the back of the page if you need to.

open	suit	rest
defeat	**un-** + **-ed**	explain
limit	button	aid

_____
_____
_____
_____
_____

Copyright Dynamic Literacy LLC   www.dynamicliteracy.com

AFFIX ADDER

Name _____

> The prefix **un-** means "not, opposite of, or absence of."
> The adjective suffix **–ed** means "having been, or made to become."

1. Write **un** in the blank space in front of each word and **ed** in the blank space after each word listed below and make a new word.
2. Tell what you think the new word means.
3. Write a sentence using the new word.

We've done one for you:
  DEFEAT means to beat in a game
  ...so UN DEFEAT ED means _not having been beaten in a game._
Sentence: _With no losses, our soccer team was undefeated last season._

1. COOK means to make fit for eating by heating up
   ...so _____COOK_____ means _____
Used in a sentence:

2. ASSIST means to help
   ...so _____ASSIST_____ means _____
Used in a sentence:

3. NAME means to give a title or label to
   ...so _____NAME_____ means _____
Used in a sentence:

4. CONCERN means to care about
   ...so _____CONCERN_____ means _____
Used in a sentence:

Copyright Dynamic Literacy LLC   www.dynamicliteracy.com

5. MELT means to grow soft by warming up
   ...so ____MELT____ means _____
Used in a sentence:

6. TEST means to check out or rate
   ...so ____TEST____ means _____
Used in a sentence:

7. FLAW means a mistake
   ...so ____FLAW____ means _____
Used in a sentence:

8. NEED means must have
   ...so ____NEED____ means _____
Used in a sentence:

9. MENTION means to say something about
   ...so ____MENTION____ means _____
Used in a sentence:

10. TRAIN means to show how to do something
    ...so ____TRAIN____ means _____
Used in a sentence:

MAGIC SQUARE

_____
Name

for **un**- meaning "not, opposite of, or absence of"
plus **-ed** meaning "having been, or made to become"

Select the best definition for each of the words in the **un** and **ed** families. Put the number of the definition in the proper space in the Magic Square box. If the numbers going up and down and the numbers going across all add up to the same thing, you have found the magic number!

WORDS
- A. uncounted
- B. unpainted
- C. unassisted
- D. untrained
- E. unseated
- F. unbuttoned
- G. unsweetened
- H. unburned
- I. unfilled

DEFINITIONS
1. not yet knowing how to do something
2. not being called by anything
3. not warm
4. not hurt by fire
5. without a coat of color
6. not complete to the top
7. not having any help
8. not closed up with round fasteners
9. not added up; without number
10. without energy
11. not having a sugary flavor
12. taken out of office; not sitting down

Magic Square Box

A.	B.	C.
D.	E.	F.
G.	H.	I.

Magic Number _____

Copyright Dynamic Literacy LLC   www.dynamicliteracy.com

Name _____

WORD SEARCH

Words with prefix un- meaning "not, opposite of, absence of"
plus suffix -ed, meaning "having been, or made to become"

Find and circle all the words in the grid. Words can go across or up and down, straight or diagonally, forwards or backwards

```
R N T F U N S I G N E D Z T R P M W U
Y M B Q Q B T T L P D Z K X H Q M P N
F Z H M N T T Y T T T N V P Q K U V W
L F T M D E D E E N N U J C R T N G A
T C U N C O N C E R N E D T D G D Z N
D M C D E T C E P X E N U J W W E D T
T P U B K K D R K D H M N N D M F E E
B T L N R U Y E E N D R C N D U E T D
D C G N C J N M N E Y U T E E N A A D
T E X R K O I T T I N M N F D M T E E
U K N Y G A O I R D A E Y Q I E E H T
X N R E L L M K O A T L T T A N D N L
J H M C P I T T E E I U P G N T Y U A
K N N E L O T K E D N N L X U I B M S
B U F N L E N W L N J V E F E O T H N
J B U G D T S U A K L N L D M N T C U
Y X J R H N E M M Q Y F N H B E U K L
Y F V Y U W E D H T N M T J D D Q K W
L J J N D D M U N L I S T E D N G R L
```

unaided	unexplained	unneeded
unclaimed	unheated	unopened
unconcerned	unlimited	unsalted
uncooked	unlisted	unsigned
undefeated	unmelted	unsweetened
undotted	unmentioned	untrained
unexpected	unnamed	unwanted

Not Made To Be!

Fill in the blanks using the words below that all mean "not having been."

Why do they mean <u>not having been</u>? _____

1. Meat that is _____ might have germs and other nasty things in it.

2. Veronica has an _____ number, so we could not call her.

3. Because the letter was _____ we didn't know who sent it.

4. Garth seemed completely _____ about getting his work done on time.

5. The mountain cabin is _____, so bring along extra blankets.

6. Tamara left _____ the fact that she wouldn't be at the game tonight.

7. Darlene and Seth could tie their shoes _____ when they were two.

8. The odd flying lights that we saw last year are still _____ to this day.

9. The snow is _____ on the mountainside that gets no sun.

10. Because Fritz doesn't know anything about cars, he is _____ for the job at the garage.

<u>Check off these words as you use them.</u>

unaided	uncooked	unheated	unmelted	unsigned
unconcerned	unexplained	unlisted	unmentioned	unsuited

SUFFIX SQUARE

Name _____

for -ly meaning "how or in what way something is done"

Start in the middle square with the suffix **ly** and combine this part with the words in the other squares to build new words. Write each word and a definition you can think of for it in the spaces provided at the bottom of the page. Use the back of the page if you need to.

fair	common	conscious
intelligent	**-ly**	sensitive
valid	certain	important

_____
_____
_____
_____
_____

Copyright Dynamic Literacy LLC   www.dynamicliteracy.com

AFFIX ADDER

_____
Name

This suffix -ly means "how or in what way something is done."

1. Write **ly** in the blank space after each word listed below and make a new word.
2. Tell what you think the new word means.
3. Write a sentence using the new word.

We've done one for you:

   CORRECT means free from error
   ...so CORRECT<u>ly</u> means <u>so as to be free from error.</u>

Sentence: <u>Lindace was careful to correctly bubble in every answer.</u>

---

1. HONEST means truthful
   ...so HONEST____ means _____
   Used in a sentence:

2. CLEAR means easy to understand
   ...so CLEAR ___ means _____
   Used in a sentence:

3. COMMON means ordinary
   ...so COMMON____ means _____
   Used in a sentence:

4. FORTUNATE means lucky
   ...so FORTUNATE____ means _____
   Used in a sentence:

Copyright Dynamic Literacy LLC   www.dynamicliteracy.com

5. **HELPFUL** means willing to assist another
    …so HELPFUL____ means _____
Used in a sentence:

6. **IMPORTANT** means of great consequence
    …so IMPORTANT____ means _____
Used in a sentence:

7. **KIND** means nice, polite
    …so KIND ____ means _____
Used in a sentence:

8. **QUIET** means without sound
    …so QUIET____ means _____
Used in a sentence:

9. **SAFE** means without danger
    …so SAFE____ means _____
Used in a sentence:

10. **WISE** means sensible; smart
    …so WISE____ means _____
Used in a sentence:

MAGIC SQUARE

_____
Name

for -ly meaning "how or in what way something is done"

Select the best definition for each of the words in the **ly** (adverb) family. Put the number of the definition in the proper space in the Magic Square box. If the numbers going up and down and the numbers going across all add up to the same thing, you have found the magic number!

WORDS
- A. intelligently
- B. commonly
- C. greatly
- D. loudly
- E. quickly
- F. naturally
- G. gradually
- H. accurately
- I. badly

DEFINITIONS
1. in a mean and nasty way
2. in a smart or knowledgeable way
3. in a way that is not good
4. in a fast way
5. in a correct way
6. in a noisy way
7. in a big way
8. in a real and not man-made way
9. in an ordinary way
10. in steps, little by little

Magic Square Box

A.	B.	C.
D.	E.	F.
G.	H.	I.

Magic Number _____

Copyright Dynamic Literacy LLC   www.dynamicliteracy.com

WORD SEARCH

Words with the suffix -ly, meaning "how or in what way a thing is done"

Find and circle all the words in the grid. Words can go across or up and down, straight or diagonally, forwards or backwards.

```
Y C O M P L E T E L Y C J K C J M B
L J H L G R T R C C O K F Y M K Y R
T Y L T N E L I S M N M X M R L L N
E Z X T V L K Y M R K T C D L D D N
I S Y R C G M O L V C K H Z D L I D
U E L N Z T N B E A U T I F U L L Y
Q N T D D L Y L L U F K N A H T A L
F S N K Y L S U O I C S N O C T V Y
A I E L K D P L N G R A D U A L L Y
I T G K Y L E N K L S Y Q B R T K Y
R I I Y V L P L T N L U P L N J L F
L V L Y L W L R I L I L D A F D B Q
Y E L H K E P U A C L C T D U Q U X
M L E M K G V R F H A R E O E I L V
P Y T Q N N U I K E O T L L C N T Y
G N N D H T C M T P E Z E K Y R L N
T T I M A L G F M C R L L L D M J Y
P K W N M D T I D M A Y G V Y C X G
```

actively	gleefully	quickly
beautifully	gradually	quietly
commonly	importantly	sensitively
completely	intelligently	silently
consciously	loudly	suddenly
delicately	naturally	thankfully
fairly	nicely	validly

_____
Name

Do It Like This

Fill in the blanks using the words below that all mean "how or in what way something is done." Why do they mean <u>how or in what way something is done</u>?

_____

1. If you live your life _____ you will stay in good shape.

2. Talking _____ during a movie is rude.

3. Everyone wants to be treated _____.

4. If you finish your homework _____ we will have time to go out for ice cream.

5. It is easier to understand a person who speaks _____ than one who mumbles.

6. Speaking _____ during a movie is considerate of other people.

7. The teacher _____ smiled at Paulette when she got the right answer.

8. Look both ways first in order to cross the street _____.

9. Spend your money _____ if you don't want to run out.

10. Accidents can happen _____ and without warning.

<u>Check off these words as you use them</u>.

kindly	loudly	suddenly	safely	wisely
actively	quickly	clearly	quietly	fairly

SUFFIX SQUARE

Name _____

for -**less** meaning "without; not having"
plus –**ly** meaning "how or in what way something is done"

Start in the middle square with the suffixes **less** and **ly** and combine these two parts with the words in the other squares to build new words. Write each word and a definition you can think of for it in the spaces provided at the bottom of the page. Use the back of the page if you need to.

help	mind	self
care	-less + -ly	harm
tact	sense	rest

_____
_____
_____
_____
_____
_____

Copyright Dynamic Literacy LLC   www.dynamicliteracy.com

AFFIX ADDER

Name _____

The suffix -less means "without; not having."

The suffix –ly means "how or in what way something is done."

1. Write **less** and **ly** in the blank spaces after each word listed below and make a new word.
2. Tell what you think the new word means.
3. Write a sentence using the new word.

We've done one for you:
   EFFORT means a struggle
   ...so EFFORT_LESS_ _LY_ means _without a struggle._
Sentence: _Clevis played the difficult song effortlessly._

___

1. CARE means concern
   ...so CARE_____ ____ means_____
Used in a sentence:

___

2. TIRE means to become fatigued
   ...so TIRE_____ ____ means _____
Used in a sentence:

___

3. FEAR means to be afraid
   ...so FEAR_____ ____ means _____
Used in a sentence:

___

4. PAIN means suffering or distress
   ...so PAIN_____ ____ means _____
Used in a sentence:

___

Copyright Dynamic Literacy LLC   www.dynamicliteracy.com

5. HARM means to injure
   ...so HARM_____ ____ means _____
   Used in a sentence:

6. JOY means happiness and pleasure
   ...so JOY_____ ____ means _____
   Used in a sentence:

7. SENSE means meaning or perception
   ...so SENSE_____ ____ means _____
   Used in a sentence:

8. NEED means requirement or necessity
   ...so NEED_____ ____ means _____
   Used in a sentence:

9. THANK means to express appreciation
   ...so THANK _____ ____ means _____
   Used in a sentence:

10. TACT means the perfect touch
    ...so TACT_____ ____ means _____
    Used in a sentence:

Copyright Dynamic Literacy LLC   www.dynamicliteracy.com

MAGIC SQUARE

_____
Name

for **-less** meaning "without; not having"

plus **-ly** meaning "how or in what way something is done"

Select the best definition for each of the words in the **less** plus **ly** family. Put the number of the definition in the proper space in the Magic Square box. If the numbers going up and down and the numbers going across all add up to the same thing, you have found the magic number!

WORDS
- A. aimlessly
- B. breathlessly
- C. speechlessly
- D. spotlessly
- E. tastelessly
- F. shamelessly
- G. lawlessly
- H. effortlessly
- I. soundlessly

DEFINITIONS
1. with no anger
2. without the ability to speak
3. without hard work
4. without any dirt or mess
5. without a sense of what is legal
6. without a sense of guilt
7. without the ability to breathe
8. without a sense of class or refinement
9. with no particular purpose or goal
10. with no noise at all

Magic Square Box

A.	B.	C.
D.	E.	F.
G.	H.	I.

Magic Number _____

Copyright Dynamic Literacy LLC

www.dynamicliteracy.com

Name _____

WORD SEARCH

Words with suffix -less, meaning "without; not having," plus -ly, meaning "how or in what way something is done."

Find and circle all the words in the grid. Words can go across or up and down, straight or diagonally, forwards or backwards.

```
E F F O R T L E S S L Y C C W Q M W L Z
L T T F B T J Y M W H Y K L J Y Y O N H
I Q R H N G K R L R L D Y P L M L R M R
F T H T O V T N R S D L R S O E S D F T
E I F U T U H G S X S Y S T N N S L G Q
L M H F M M G E K S R E I D P W E E Y L
E E M R V O L H E N L O L X T B L S T Y
S L Q D D P R L T E N E R T T Q H S Q L
S E R N L N E L S L S Y H R N F T L Y S
L S R E M P Y A E S E K P X K I R Y L S
Y S H W A M E S L S N S K Q L K O H S E
L L L H R C S Y C M S R S L T N W P S L
M Y S H L L Y C V M L L R L W M V P E N
N T K B Y L B X Z J N M Y N Y K Q K L O
N Y M D E F E N S E L E S S L Y M J F I
Z K T C N Q K Y L S S E L E M A N W L T
K H E A R T L E S S L Y M R Q Y D N E O
T H A N K L E S S L Y Y T X T V N L S M
P M M M Y L S S E L E R A C Z H D T J E
P Y U S E L E S S L Y Q F W G K R N W P
```

carelessly	helplessly	shapelessly
ceaselessly	humorlessly	thanklessly
defenselessly	lifelessly	thoughtlessly
effortlessly	motionlessly	timelessly
emotionlessly	namelessly	uselessly
endlessly	pointlessly	wordlessly
heartlessly	selflessly	worthlessly

In a Manner with Less

Fill in the blanks using the words below that all mean "done without having."

Why do they mean <u>done without having</u>? _____

1. Beowulf was brave. He _____ faced and fought the monster and the dragon.

2. Mr. Albert did not give his name when he made the donation. He made the donation _____.

3. Darrell didn't have any reason to be out in the hall. He was just _____ walking around out there.

4. Rodney was speaking very _____, so we could not tell if he was happy or sad.

5. It was Karen's birthday, so she happily and _____ ate two pieces of cake.

6. We couldn't do anything about the storm knocking out our lights. We waited _____ until the electricity could be restored.

7. Twarn slept peacefully and _____ after his hard day of work.

8. The sled flew down the icy hill _____.

9. The thief entered the room _____ and stole my watch.

10. Wendy and Eleu worked _____ until they finished the job.

<u>Check off these words as you use them.</u>

| dreamlessly | fearlessly | guiltlessly | noiselessly | purposelessly |
| emotionlessly | frictionlessly | namelessly | powerlessly | tirelessly |

SUFFIX SQUARE

Name _____

for -y meaning "tending to have or be like"

Start in the middle square with the suffix **y** and combine this part with the words in the other squares to build new words. Write each word and a definition you can think of for it in the spaces provided at the bottom of the page. Use the back of the page if you need to.

snow	rain	cloud
chill	-y	trick
luck	dirt	foam

_____
_____
_____
_____
_____
_____
_____

Copyright Dynamic Literacy LLC

www.dynamicliteracy.com

AFFIX ADDER

_____
Name

The suffix **-y** means "tending to have or be like."

1. Write **y** in the blank space after each word listed below and make a new word.
2. Tell what you think the new word means.
3. Write a sentence using the new word.

We've done one for you:

CLOUD is a condensation of moisture in the sky
...so CLOUD**y** means <u>tending to be like moisture in the sky.</u>
Sentence: The forecast says that the day will be cloudy.

_____

1. CURL means to twist into ringlets
   ...so CURL__ means _____

_____

2. CHEER means happiness
   ...so CHEER__ means _____

_____

3. FUSS means to be nervous about or to worry over minor things
   ...so FUSS__ means _____

_____

4. SPEED means rapid movement
   ...so SPEED__ means _____

Copyright Dynamic Literacy LLC   www.dynamicliteracy.com

5. TRICK means to deceive or fool someone
   ...so TRICK___ means _____

6. LUCK refers to good fortune
   ...so LUCK ___ means _____

7. ITCH refers to irritation on the skin
   ...so ITCH___ means _____

8. DUSK refers to twilight or sunset
   ...so DUSK ___ means _____

9. WEED refers to a grassy plant that grows where it is not wanted
   ...so WEED___ means _____

10. SNOW refers to fluffy, white precipitation
    ...so SNOW___ means _____

MAGIC SQUARE

_____
Name

for **-y** meaning "tending to have or be like"

Select the best definition for each of the words in the suffix **y** family. Put the number of the definition in the proper space in the Magic Square box. If the numbers going up and down and the numbers going across all add up to the same thing, you have found the magic number!

WORDS
- A. silky
- B. woodsy
- C. lengthy
- D. roomy
- E. glassy
- F. boxy
- G. messy
- H. sleepy
- I. grassy

DEFINITIONS
1. too long or complicated; not brief
2. with the quality of trees or forests
3. tending to have low, green growth
4. having plenty of space
5. jumbled and unarranged
6. shiny and easy to see through
7. tending to be long
8. having a simple and square quality
9. feeling soft and smooth
10. tired and ready for bed

Magic Square Box

A.	B.	C.
D.	E.	F.
G.	H.	I.

Magic Number _____

Copyright Dynamic Literacy LLC   www.dynamicliteracy.com

Name _____

WORD SEARCH

Words with the suffix -y, meaning "tending to have or be like"

Find and circle all the words in the grid. Words can go across or up and down, straight or diagonally, forwards or backwards.

```
R D R M U S H Y C K J N K R
G U T N R Y K Y V K J N Q Y
R S Y X L C M N R Y G Y R H
E K L R I B T R C F X D A C
E Y U R N M W O H H G U I U
D C T F O Y T H Y N I O N O
Y L T O X M G T Y T L L Y R
H F D M Y T M L M T A C L G
H Y U H F L U C K Y L E K Y
X A C S F D I R T Y N I W N
F T I O S Y F O O G B R U S
I X A R L Y L Q Z J V K M G
R M Y B Y R T J R T T F J M
Y H X C Q Y D E E P S K B Z
```

chilly	goofy	moody
cloudy	greedy	mushy
curly	grouchy	rainy
dirty	guilty	speedy
dusky	hairy	sweaty
foamy	itchy	thorny
fussy	lucky	tricky

Name _____

Made Up Of!

Fill in the blanks using the words at the bottom of the page that all mean "tending to have or be like."

Why do they mean tending to have or be like something? because of the suffix y

1. Drive-through service is a _____ way to get things done.

2. The _____ garden needed much better care.

3. Even on a _____ day you can get a sunburn.

4. The _____ old man angrily chased the kids off his property.

5. Because he felt _____, Zeke bought three tickets for the Charity Drawing.

6. It was so _____ and cold that we could not travel very fast or far.

7. The _____ kids did not put away their toys when they were finished.

8. Becci said her ankles were getting _____ after she walked through the poison ivy.

9. The clouds looked so soft and _____ that we imagined resting in them.

10. Riding a bike safely through heavy traffic can be a _____ experience.

Check off these words as you use them.

| cloudy | foamy | fussy | itchy | lucky |
| messy | snowy | speedy | tricky | weedy |

Copyright Dynamic Literacy LLC

www.dynamicliteracy.com

SUFFIX SQUARE

_____
Name

for –y changed to –i meaning "tending to have or be like"

plus –ness meaning "quality or condition"

Start in the middle square with the suffixes **y** changed to **i** and **ness** and combine these parts with the words in the other squares to build new words. Write each word and a definition you can think of for it in the spaces provided at the bottom of the page. Use the back of the page if you need to.

curl	dirt	speed
sweat	-y to -i + -ness	luck
guilt	goof	thirst

_____
_____
_____
_____

Copyright Dynamic Literacy LLC

www.dynamicliteracy.com

AFFIX ADDER

_____
Name

> The suffix **-y** means "tending to have or be like."
> The suffix **–ness** means "quality or condition."
> When **ness** is attached to a word ending with the suffix **y**, the final **y** is almost always dropped and replaced with **i**.

1. Draw a line through the final letter **y** of each of the words below.
2. Write **i** and **ness** in the blank spaces after each word listed below and make a new word.
3. Tell what you think the new word means.
4. Write a sentence using the new word.

We've done one for you:
   THRIFTY means tending to save money through careful spending
   ...so THRIFT̶Y̶ _i_ _NESS_ means _quality of tending to save money through careful spending._

Sentence: _The habit of thriftiness has created many a wealthy person._
_____

1. CHEERY means tending to be happy
   ...so CHEERY__ _____ means _____

   _____

2. LUCKY means tending to have good fortune
   ...so LUCKY__ _____ means _____

   _____

3. GREEDY means tending to want more than one's fair share
   ...so GREEDY__ _____ means _____

   _____

Copyright Dynamic Literacy LLC   www.dynamicliteracy.com

4. **DUSKY** means like the half light at sunset
   ...so DUSKY__ _____ means _____

5. **GROUCHY** means tending to be bad tempered
   ...so GROUCHY__ _____ means _____

6. **WORTHY** means tending to be deserving
   ...so WORTHY__ _____ means _____

7. **THIRSTY** means tending to be in need of something to drink
   ...so THIRSTY__ _____ means _____

8. **MOODY** means tending to be unhappy or uneven in feelings
   ...so MOODY__ _____ means _____

9. **WEEDY** tending to be overgrown with undesirable plants
   ...so WEEDY __ _____ means _____

10. **GUILTY** means to have responsibility for a crime
    ...so GUILTY__ _____ means _____

MAGIC SQUARE

_____
Name

for –y changed to -i meaning "tending to have or be like"

plus –ness meaning "quality or condition"

Select the best definition for each of the words in the **y** changed to **i** plus **ness** family. Put the number of the definition in the proper space in the Magic Square box. If the numbers going up and down and the numbers going across all add up to the same thing, you have found the magic number!

WORDS
- A. raininess
- B. cloudiness
- C. spookiness
- D. chilliness
- E. trickiness
- F. thorniness
- G. silkiness
- H. itchiness
- I. worthiness

DEFINITIONS
1. tending to demand some degree of attention
2. sky conditions that blocks the sun
3. condition of being soft and smooth
4. quality of having sharp spines
5. quality of being valuable or full of honor
6. quality of fooling or playing jokes
7. state of weather made up of water falling from the sky
8. quality of being cold
9. quality of being scary
10. quality of feeling tingly or scratchy

Magic Square Box

A.	B.	C.
D.	E.	F.
G.	H.	I.

Magic Number _____

Copyright Dynamic Literacy LLC   www.dynamicliteracy.com

Name _____

WORD SEARCH

Words with the suffix -y changed to -i, meaning "tending to have or be like" plus -ness, meaning "quality or condition"

Find and circle all the words in the grid. Words can go across or up and down, straight or diagonally, forwards or backwards

```
W V T R K K C V R S S E N I L L I H C W
F S S E N I D E E W M O O D I N E S S F
Y Q P Z R N R T P M Z H V M J F R G P M
P T D H T M P X R B B G H B B B R T E S
T B E B S G R E E D I N E S S T R L E S
R H W L P P D B G L N R N T P J U V D E
S M I D B K O Q W S R O A Z L C C J I N
K S N R Y Z N O S N W R H I K T S K N I
F M E Q S X T E K I W L F I N R S J E D
M M S N K T N H N I R H N X S I E W S U
N Z S F I I I E Y S N E G S Y C N Q S O
N C B Q H T S N S S S E E K D K I E S L
T R P S J S F E E S S N S M C I H Q S C
W W U H K Q N I G S I E X S Z N T T E S
H M K T G I L D R L S D N P L E R Q N K
F C Q H T P Y T R H M Q Z I Z S O G I C
Z R J R N P H U L L T R H B F S W K H Y
M T I Z Q L C T D W F V M R C O Z L C V
T D W B N J F U S S I N E S S Z O R T G
J Q N D B T Q R C T K T M R Y C C G I R
```

chilliness	greediness	speediness
cloudiness	itchiness	spookiness
curliness	luckiness	thirstiness
dewiness	moodiness	thriftiness
dirtiness	mushiness	trickiness
fussiness	raininess	weediness
goofiness	snowiness	worthiness

Name _____

It's Like This…

Fill in the blanks using the words at the bottom of the page that all mean "tending to have or be like."

Why do they mean <u>the quality or condition of having or being like</u>?

_____

1. His _____ at the keyboard beat all the others by about 3 words per minute.

2. Steve and Stella have a hunger and _____ to learn a new language this summer.

3. Jawan's _____ at predicting winning teams is incredible.

4. The Funkhouser family enjoyed the _____ of the old-time comedy team.

5. Because of Ruby's _____, no one else got a piece of pie.

6. Spotting a pool of water, Mary questioned the _____ of the boat to float.

7. The _____ of Mr. Fink makes him friendly one minute and quiet the next.

8. The teacher used the _____ of roses to teach the dangers that can lurk in attractive things.

9. Francine loved to feel the _____ of her Persian cat's fur.

10. The _____ of the day meant that it would probably rain.

<u>Check off these words as you use them</u>.

| cloudiness | goofiness | greediness | luckiness | moodiness |
| silkiness | speediness | thirstiness | thorniness | worthiness |

Copyright Dynamic Literacy LLC   www.dynamicliteracy.com

SUFFIX SQUARE

Name _____

for -ly meaning "like in appearance, manner, or nature"

Start in the middle square with the suffix **ly** and combine this part with the words in the other squares to build new words. Write each word and a definition you can think of for it in the spaces provided at the bottom of the page. Use the back of the page if you need to.

brother	weak	sick
friend	**-ly**	clean
love	ghost	coward

_____
_____
_____
_____
_____
_____

Copyright Dynamic Literacy LLC   www.dynamicliteracy.com

AFFIX ADDER

_____
Name

> This suffix **-ly** means "like in appearance, manner, or nature."
>
> 1. Write **ly** in the blank space after each word listed below and make a new word.
> 2. Tell what you think the new word means.
> 3. Write a sentence using the new word.

We've done one for you:

  SICK means ill

  ...so SICK**ly** means _ill in appearance, manner, or nature._

Sentence: _Zack looked sickly, so I told him to go home and get some rest._

___

1. MISER is a person who piles up but won't spend money
   ...so MISER____ means _____

___

2. SHAPE refers to the outline of a thing
   ...so SHAPE ___ means _____

___

3. DISORDER means lacking neatness or system
   ...so DISORDER____ means _____

___

4. MONTH means a 30-day period
   ...so MONTH____ means _____

___

Copyright Dynamic Literacy LLC   www.dynamicliteracy.com

5. MANNER refers to polite ways of behaving
   ...so MANNER____ means _____

6. WEEK refers to a seven-day period
   ...so WEEK____ means _____

7. SISTER refers to one's female sibling
   ...so SISTER____ means _____

8. QUARTER refers to one-fourth of something
   ...so QUARTER____ means _____

9. FRIEND is a person you can count on and trust
   ...so FRIEND____ means _____

10. WOMAN refers to a female adult
    ...so WOMAN____ means _____

MAGIC SQUARE

_____
Name

for -ly meaning "like in appearance, manner, or nature"

Select the best definition for each of the words in the **ly** (adjective) family. Put the number of the definition in the proper space in the Magic Square box. If the numbers going up and down and the numbers going across all add up to the same thing, you have found the magic number!

WORDS
A. earthly
B. manly
C. teacherly
D. costly
E. brotherly
F. orderly
G. princely
H. friendly
I. timely

DEFINITIONS
1. like someone who hoards money
2. like an instructor or educator
3. like a nice and agreeable person
4. having a high price
5. like the son of a king or queen
6. in a patterned and neat arrangement
7. behaving like a male
8. like a male sibling
9. relating to this world
10. happening at the right moment

Magic Square Box

A.	B.	C.
D.	E.	F.
G.	H.	I.

Magic Number _____

Copyright Dynamic Literacy LLC   www.dynamicliteracy.com

Name _____

WORD SEARCH

Words with the suffix -ly, meaning "like in appearance, manner, or nature"

Find and circle all the words in the grid. Words can go across or up and down, straight or diagonally, forwards or backwards.

```
M L P M L Q K F L Y L R E H T O M K D
Y M C M T T M L T J M Z Z P V Y B R W
P N O M F C O Y P R I N C E L Y M Y M
Y Z S N R V N L M G J G L R R A L D K
J F T N E Y M H T V V N E L N E Q W L
U R L L V L N T F T R H W N M R R P K
Z N Y R T E D R X R C Q E O Y R D K M
K Y M R T M J A H A I R H L J X I M T
B C J A D I L E E L L E E C V J S Q M
L Y D D N T L T Y Y G K N K L N O G K
G L W X N N S J M L I T C D L D R X N
S N R V K U E I Y L R L R T L V D R F
H A L F L Y Z R S B P E J Q P Y E L T
A M S I C K L Y L T J Q H Y L N R K D
P N Z P X B X K J Y E L M T L Q L G R
E N D F R B R O T H E R L Y A E Y M L
L R Y K R N H M N P Z P L W H F M Z V
Y J N V J K K N J X K J F Y K M K I T
J W N K Y L R E H T A F D N A R G Y T
```

brotherly	homely	shapely
costly	likely	sickly
disorderly	lovely	sisterly
earthly	manly	teacherly
fatherly	mannerly	timely
friendly	motherly	unmannerly
grandfatherly	princely	untimely

_____
Name

Just Like it

Fill in the blanks using the words below that all mean "like in appearance, nature, or manner." Why do they mean <u>like in appearance, nature, or manner</u>?

_____

1. The bank sends out twelve _____ statements per year.

2. Homework should be done in a _____ manner.

3. New cars can be expensive, or _____.

4. A beard or moustache is a _____ characteristic.

5. A high voice is a _____ characteristic.

6. Being _____ makes it easier to meet people.

7. Being _____ makes it harder to meet people.

8. During a fire drill, you are asked to walk in an _____ fashion.

9. The _____ flowers brightened Ms. Johnson's day.

10. Fictional aliens from outer space are not _____ beings!

<u>Check off these words as you use them</u>.

| lovely | timely | friendly | orderly | costly |
| womanly | earthly | monthly | unfriendly | manly |

SUFFIX SQUARE

Name _____

for **-ship** meaning "position, status, or skill"

Start in the middle square with the suffix **ship** and combine this part with the words in the other squares to build new words. Write each word and a definition you can think of for it in the spaces provided at the bottom of the page. Use the back of the page if you need to.

author	citizen	friend
leader	**-ship**	kin
champion	sponsor	member

_____

_____

_____

_____

_____

_____

Copyright Dynamic Literacy LLC   www.dynamicliteracy.com

AFFIX ADDER

_____
Name

The suffix -ship means "position, status, or skill."

1. Write **ship** in the blank space after each word listed below and make a new word.
2. Tell what you think the new word means.
3. Write a sentence using the new word.

We've done one for you:

　　MENTOR means a guiding teacher

　　...so MENTOR _SHIP_ means _the position of a guiding teacher._

Sentence: _Under the mentorship of Mr. Kellogg, the students became experts in African culture._

---

1. DEALER means a person who sells something
　　...so DEALER _____ means _____
Used in a sentence:

2. FELLOW means a companion or friend
　　...so FELLOW_____ means _____
Used in a sentence:

3. DICTATOR means an overly powerful ruler
　　...so EMPLOY_____ means _____
Used in a sentence:

4. OWNER means a person who has something
　　...so OWNER _____ means _____
Used in a sentence:

Copyright Dynamic Literacy LLC　　　　　　　　　　　　www.dynamicliteracy.com

5. PARTNER means a co-worker or companion
   ...so PARTNER _____ means _____
   Used in a sentence:

6. RELATION means to kin or connection
   ...so RELATION _____ means _____
   Used in a sentence:

7. TRUSTEE means a person who guards and guides
   ...so TRUSTEE _____ means _____
   Used in a sentence:

8. VIEWER means a person who watches
   ...so VIEWER _____ means _____
   Used in a sentence:

9. TOWN means an area where people live as a group
   ...so TOWN _____ means _____
   Used in a sentence:

10. SPEAKER means a person in charge of talking for a group
    ...so SPEAKER _____ means _____
    Used in a sentence:

MAGIC SQUARE

_____
Name

for -ship meaning "position, status, or skill"

Select the best definition for each of the words in the **ship** family. Put the number of the definition in the proper space in the Magic Square box. If the numbers going up and down and the numbers going across all add up to the same thing, you have found the magic number!

WORDS
- A. instructorship
- B. viewership
- C. sponsorship
- D. ownership
- E. friendship
- F. championship
- G. membership
- H. dictatorship
- I. citizenship

DEFINITIONS
1. the skill of serving well in society
2. the status of liking another and being liked
3. the skill of being a teacher
4. the position of having
5. the position of being a supporter or backer
6. the position of being a domineering leader
7. the status of those who watch as a group
8. the status of belonging to a club
9. the status of being a winner

Magic Square Box

A.	B.	C.
D.	E.	F.
G.	H.	I.

Magic Number _____

Copyright Dynamic Literacy LLC   www.dynamicliteracy.com

WORD SEARCH

Words with the suffix -ship, meaning "position, status, or skill."

Find and circle all the words in the grid. Words can go across or up and down, straight or diagonally, forwards or backwards.

```
T Y M K W J W K Q P I H S R E N T R A P H
C D G Q D M Y V I E W E R S H I P P G R R
P I H S W O L L E F L T Z D Q B Y C N T D
I P X K L E A D E R S H I P W P N Z T I V
H I M N Y Q P I H S R E K A E P S W C T Y
S H E P I H S R O S N O P S M T F T K W K
R S N C H A M P I O N S H I P N A F L T P
O N T N T R V H C N P W R B H T W V L I T
T O O L C M K Y B I F I D V O R L D H W R
C I R X G P E N V T T P H R M Y B S T P R
U T S R M I Y M K P L I S S M R N L I D L
R A H B D H B R B L I H Z H N A R H L H R
T L I G E S F T X E I H P E S W S T B J O
S E P N A R J Z D P R I S I N E O W P W P
N R R W L O K Y W V H S T D E S R T N N H
I D Q B E H T M X S K R H T N Y H E Z M R
L K L C R T L Q N R A W S I Q E R I Z Q R
C H X T S U G I N P R U X L P S I B P Y G
G C R N H A K X I J R D B B H Q F R Z N N
H D R W I H Q B T T V C L I W P R L F N R
B T Q C P P C M C H M H P L L K Y R J T T
```

authorship	friendship	partnership
bipartisanship	instructorship	relationship
championship	kinship	speakership
citizenship	leadership	sponsorship
dealership	membership	township
dictatorship	mentorship	trusteeship
fellowship	ownership	viewership

Name _____

Ship Shape!

Fill in the blanks using the words below that all mean "position, status, or skill at something."
Why do they mean position, status, or skill at something? _____

1. Under the guiding _____ of Mrs. Rice, the teenager became an excellent writer.

2. Marsha went into _____ with her father to form a family business.

3. For the marathon, Jude had the supportive _____ of four companies.

4. The _____ of that television show consists of kids between 5 and 8.

5. The _____ of the stories which we read is not known.

6. Kyle and Kira have enjoyed a warm and close _____ for ten years.

7. Under Tommy's _____, the school raised a thousand dollars for the disaster relief.

8. Danielle passed her test for _____ of the United States.

9. The brother and sister share _____ of the farm where they were born.

10. Do you know the _____ that the English language has with Latin?

Check off these words as you use them.

| authorship | citizenship | friendship | leadership | mentorship |
| ownership | partnership | relationship | sponsorship | viewership |

Copyright Dynamic Literacy LLC   www.dynamicliteracy.com

SUFFIX SQUARE

Name _____

for –y changed to -i meaning "being like or having"

plus –ly meaning "how or in what way something is done"

Start in the middle square with the suffixes **y** (changed to **i**) and **ly**. Combine these parts with the words in the other squares to build new words. Write each word and a definition you can think of for it in the spaces provided at the bottom of the page. Use the back of the page if you need to.

luck	heart	sneak
thrift	-y to -i + -ly	worth
greed	dream	thirst

_____
_____
_____
_____
_____

Copyright Dynamic Literacy LLC   www.dynamicliteracy.com

AFFIX ADDER

_____
Name

> The suffix **-y**, meaning "being like or having," changes to **-i** before the suffix **-ly**, meaning
> "how or in what way something is done."

1. Cross out the ending **y** of each of the following words and replace it with an **i** in the space that follows.
2. Write **ly** in the blank space after each **i** and make a new word.
3. Tell what you think the new word means.
4. Write a sentence using the new word.

We've done one for you:
    BUSY means being active and having lots to do
    ...so BUS~~Y~~ _i_ _LY_ means _in a very active way having lots to do._
Sentence: _The students worked busily all day making their Word Wall._

1. HAPPY means glad and cheerful
   ...so HAPPY__ ____ means_____
Used in a sentence:

2. EASY means not hard to do
   ...so EASY __ ____ means _____
Used in a sentence:

3. SPEEDY means fast
   ...so SPEEDY __ ____ means _____
Used in a sentence:

4. WEARY means tired
   ...so WEARY __ ____ means _____
Used in a sentence:

Copyright Dynamic Literacy LLC   www.dynamicliteracy.com

5. ANGRY means mad

   ...so ANGRY __ _____ means _____

   Used in a sentence:

6. HASTY means too quick

   ...so HASTY __ _____ means _____

   Used in a sentence:

7. CLUMSY means awkward

   ...so CLUMSY __ _____ means _____

   Used in a sentence:

8. NOISY means loud

   ...so NOISY __ _____ means _____

   Used in a sentence:

9. THRIFTY means careful with money or goods

   ...so THRIFTY __ _____ means _____

   Used in a sentence:

10. STEADY means firm or without interruption

    ...so STEADY __ _____ means _____

    Used in a sentence:

Copyright Dynamic Literacy LLC   www.dynamicliteracy.com

MAGIC SQUARE

_____
Name

for -y changed to -i meaning "being like or having"
plus -ly meaning "how or in what way something is done"

Select the best definition for each of the words in the **y** to **i** plus **ly** family. Put the number of the definition in the proper space in the Magic Square box. If the numbers going up and down and the numbers going across all add up to the same thing, you have found the magic number!

WORDS
A. sleepily
B. daintily
C. heavily
D. lazily
E. militarily
F. sturdily
G. sneakily
H. worthily
I. hastily

DEFINITIONS
1. in a manner of saving money
2. so as to be delicate or pretty
3. so as to hurry
4. in a manner not wanting to work
5. in a manner of trying to hide something
6. in a manner of armed forces
7. so as to be serious or full of weight
8. so as to be firm
9. in a manner of not being fully awake
10. so as to be respected or have value

Magic Square Box

A.	B.	C.
D.	E.	F.
G.	H.	I.

Magic Number _____

Copyright Dynamic Literacy LLC   www.dynamicliteracy.com

Name _____

WORD SEARCH

Words with the suffix -y changed to -i, meaning "being like or having," plus suffix -ly, meaning "like, being."

Find and circle all the words in the grid. Words can go across or up and down, straight or diagonally, forwards or backwards.

```
L M M S T E A D I L Y Z F M P K G D
G N T N Y L I S A E L Z Q M Z T R M
P D K P Y M P N Y Q I P T T K O Y T
X Q Z M G Y K L M B R T V W W R L H
L T R F V W I N Y W G K K S D X I R
A Z Q D P P Y F N L N H I X F D D I
Z W R V E L N C N L A L Z T Y F E F
I V N E I K C P U Y Y C C N L J E T
L Y L T F T T C L C W L L H I M P I
Y S S K L Z K I D X Y O I M P V S L
N A R M N I S D T A Q L R K P T X Y
H N L G L U K R R N I H I T A B K V
X T Z Y B V G E Y X M N E D H E R X
G N R V R K R A Q K D T T A E I N T
P K K L C L U M S I L Y M I V E L S
F J W K P Q X I H R C K F W L I R Y
C H E A R T I L Y H B V D Z N Y L G
T B L K P G V Y V P Y L I S I O N Y
```

angrily	greedily	noisily
busily	happily	sleepily
clumsily	hastily	sneakily
daintily	heartily	speedily
dreamily	heavily	steadily
drowsily	lazily	thriftily
easily	luckily	worthily

Mind your Manners!

Fill in the blanks using the words below that all mean "in a manner of or so as to be something."
Why do they mean <u>in a manner of or so as to be something</u>?

_____

1. People who know about prefixes can _____ spell the word **misspell**.

2. At the reunion, a smiling Ms. Thresh _____ greeted her former students.

3. The magician _____ moved the card from one hand to the other.

4. It snowed _____ for two days without any let-up.

5. Ru _____ saves paper bags to reuse for her lunch.

6. Igor _____ slammed on the desk and demanded an answer.

7. Paddy _____ took three pieces of cake, leaving none for the rest of us.

8. Elvira was _____ not hurt when a driver ran a red light and hit her car.

9. The firefighters raced _____ to get to the burning house.

10. Reba worked so _____ that she didn't realize how much time had passed.

<u>Check off these words as you use them</u>.

| angrily | busily | easily | greedily | happily |
| luckily | sneakily | speedily | steadily | thriftily |

PREFIX SQUARE

_____
Name

for **mis-** meaning "badly or wrong"

Start in the middle square with the prefix **mis** and combine this part with the words in the other squares to build new words. Write each word and a definition you can think of for it in the spaces provided at the bottom of the page. Use the back of the page if you need to.

fit	take	cast
lead	**mis-**	step
use	file	cue

_____

_____

_____

_____

_____

Copyright Dynamic Literacy LLC   www.dynamicliteracy.com

AFFIX ADDER

_____
Name

The prefix **mis-** means "badly or wrong."

1. Write **mis** in the blank space in front of each word listed below and make a new word.
2. Tell what you think the new word means.
3. Write a sentence using the new word.

We've done one for you:

  FIT means to suit or be proper
  ...so MISFIT means <u>badly suited.</u>

Sentence: The role of elf in the school play misfit Ed because he is so tall.

_____

1. BELIEVE means to take as true or right
   ...so ____BELIEVE means _____
Used in a sentence:

_____

2. CAST means to hire the actors that will be in a play or movie
   ...so ____CAST means _____
Used in a sentence:

_____

3. CUE is a hint
   ...so ____CUE means _____
Used in a sentence:

_____

4. STEP is a move in a certain direction
   ...so ____STEP means _____
Used in a sentence:

_____

5. TELL means to say or to speak something
   ...so ____TELL means _____
Used in a sentence:

6. TAKE means to interpret or understand in a certain way
   ...so ____TAKE means _____
Used in a sentence:

7. FILE means to put in place
   ...so ____FILE means _____
Used in a sentence:

8. STATE means to voice facts or opinions
   ...so ____STATE means _____
Used in a sentence:

9. LEAD is to show the way
   ...so ____LEAD means _____
Used in a sentence:

10. FIRE means to pull the trigger on a gun
    ...so ____FIRE means _____
Used in a sentence:

MAGIC SQUARE

_____
Name

for **mis**- meaning "badly or wrong"

Select the best definition for each of the words in the **mis** family. Put the number of the definition in the proper space in the Magic Square box. If the numbers going up and down and the numbers going across all add up to the same thing, you have found the magic number!

WORDS
- A. misunderstand
- B. mislocate
- C. misaddress
- D. misadvise
- E. misword
- F. mislabel
- G. misplay
- H. misspell
- I. misbehave

DEFINITIONS
1. to act in a bad way
2. to say in the wrong way
3. to believe or hear in the wrong way
4. to tell someone to do something that is in error
5. to send a letter to the wrong person or place
6. to say the wrong letters of a word
7. to lose or misplace
8. to make the wrong move in a game
9. to put the wrong tag or name onto

Magic Square Box

A.	B.	C.
D.	E.	F.
G.	H.	I.

Magic Number _____

Copyright Dynamic Literacy LLC   www.dynamicliteracy.com

Name _____

WORD SEARCH

Words with the prefix mis- meaning "badly or wrong"

Find and circle the words in the grid. Words can go across or up and down, straight or diagonally, forwards or backwards

```
P L L N M D N E S S I M Z Q K V B
Q E B E H Z M K K J M C D D V R L
Z N T J V M K M K T Q I R C T V M
N M K S R I I F K P W O S G D T I
I L I D S S G M Z O W V T L D K S
O M B S C I L S N S K Q I M E T A
J N D U A N M K I N P M F H Y A D
S K E X F I S M K M M I S L A Y D
I V G N R I M P I K J S I T Z L R
M M F R M B M S R R R C M V M E E
W I K K M P P E L H Z A C X C S S
Y S R D L L R N A L P S I M X U S
Z T G K A I M K H X F T Y V L S P
M A X Y F M I S B E L I E V E I T
Z K B S P M H E L I F S I M K M L
N E I M M I S A D V I S E L D T W
J M H N N B R Y N Q K C C K J H H
```

misaddress	misfire	misplan
misadvise	misfit	misplay
misaim	misgive	missend
misbelieve	misjoin	misstep
miscast	misknow	mistake
miscue	mislay	misuse
misfile	mislead	misword

Name _____

Wrong!

Fill in the blanks using the words below that all mean "to do something badly or wrong." Why do they mean <u>to do something badly or wrong</u>? _____

1. Because she knows word roots, Shauna rarely _____ words.

2. You didn't do the project correctly. Did you _____ the instructions?

3. When the teacher had to leave the room, the good students didn't _____.

4. A few of the Fourth of July rockets _____ or did not go off at all.

5. Absent-minded Andi always _____ his reading glasses.

6. The game director called a _____ and took away our points.

7. Be careful not to _____ when getting off an escalator.

8. From weeks of _____, the printer finally stopped working.

9. Jo must have _____ the report under the letter A instead of B.

10. Mr. Hogan said he didn't want to _____ us into thinking the wrong thing.

<u>Check off these words as you use them</u>.

misbehave	misfiled	misfired	mislead	mislocates
misplay	misspells	misstep	misunderstand	misuse

SUFFIX SQUARE

_____
Name

for -**some** meaning "the same as or like something"

Start in the middle square with the suffix **some** and combine this part with the words in the other squares to build new words. Write each word and a definition you can think of for it in the spaces provided at the bottom of the page. Use the back of the page if you need to.

bother	fear	awe
toil	-**some**	trouble
whole	tire	flavor

_____
_____
_____
_____
_____

Copyright Dynamic Literacy LLC   www.dynamicliteracy.com

AFFIX ADDER

_____
Name

> **The suffix -some means "the same as or like something."**
>
> 1. Write **some** in the blank space after each word listed below and make a new word.
> 2. Tell what you think the new word means.
> 3. Write a sentence using the new word.

We've done one for you:

   AWE is an overwhelming emotional feeling
   ...so AWE<u>SOME</u> means _like an overwhelming emotional feeling._

Sentence: _The beautiful sunset last evening was awesome._

---

1. BURDEN means something difficult to stand or endure
   ...so BURDEN_____ means _____

2. BOTHER means to disturb or annoy
   ...so BOTHER _____ means _____

3. FEAR means a feeling of being scared
   ...so FEAR_____ means _____

4. FROLIC means to act playfully
   ...so FROLIC_____ means _____

Copyright Dynamic Literacy LLC   www.dynamicliteracy.com

5. IRK means to irritate mildly
   ...so IRK_____ means _____

6. LONE means by yourself with no companion
   ...so LONE_____ means _____

7. QUARREL means to argue
   ...so QUARREL_____ means _____

8. WHOLE means complete, missing nothing essential
   ...so WHOLE_____ means _____

9. WOE means distress or misery
   ...so WOE _____ means _____

10. BUNGLE means to mess up or handle badly
    ...so BUNGLE_____ means _____

MAGIC SQUARE

_____
Name

for **-some** meaning "the same as or like something"

Select the best definition for each of the words in the suffix **some** family. Put the number of the definition in the proper space in the Magic Square box. If the numbers going up and down and the numbers going across all add up to the same thing, you have found the magic number!

WORDS
- A. boresome
- B. twosome
- C. toothsome
- D. burdensome
- E. quarrelsome
- F. playsome
- G. meddlesome
- H. mannersome
- I. lonesome

DEFINITIONS
1. charming and affectionate
2. very uninteresting
3. missing the company of other people
4. arguing or complaining
5. very polite
6. heavy or hard to do
7. pleasing to bite into or to taste
8. known for having fun or making jokes
9. a pair of players or partners
10. getting in the middle of other people's business

Magic Square Box

A.	B.	C.
D.	E.	F.
G.	H.	I.

Magic Number _____

Copyright Dynamic Literacy LLC   www.dynamicliteracy.com

Name _____

WORD SEARCH

Words with the suffix -some, meaning "the same as or like something"

Find and circle all the words in the grid. Words can go across or up and down, straight or diagonally, forwards or backwards.

```
J T N L D E M O S L I O T H N J T T L
U N W H O L E S O M E F X Z F H M M M
F T I R E S O M E M M T Y L R W L W E
T T Q J K Q Y W O H V G P E B H T T M
M K R M F M M S B U R D E N S O M E O
F W M O K J E G D B T S K L E L B Z S
E O M N U W J L V E O H M G M E U L H
A E N E A B T F M M E T F Q O S N W T
R S E N M J L O E M V R H M S O G G A
S O H M M O S E O Y O E V E E M L M O
O M N N O R S S S L W M X M R E E R L
M E W M O S L E I O J O W P U S S N G
E D Y V M E E C N X M S V R T W O K N
V D A X R Q S R Y O Q E D Z N H M M R
N L X R D O V R U Z L L H M E M E L E
F Z A P M M B Y C T Q D L N V H V N K
T U T E N B N Q L R N D H M D T H K L
Q H H T T P C Z N K Z E D B A Q J C T
H M X E M O S K R I Q M V D L N Z T B
```

adventuresome	frolicsome	tiresome
awesome	irksome	toilsome
bothersome	loathsome	troublesome
bunglesome	lonesome	unwholesome
burdensome	meddlesome	venturesome
fearsome	quarrelsome	wholesome
flavorsome	threesome	woesome

It's Like this….

Fill in the blanks using the words at the bottom of the page that all mean "the same as or like something."
Why do they mean the same as or like something? _____

1. Cinderella led a _____ life. She had to do all the work around the house.

2. Josh has a _____, healthy smile.

3. Some left their country for freedom, but others were simply _____.

4. Taking on the workload of my sick coworker has been a _____ task.

5. Jody laughed to watch the _____ otters playing in the water.

6. The _____ stranger sitting next to me kept asking personal questions.

7. Weezie is very _____. She picks arguments for no good reason.

8. The chocolate-covered ants were actually quite _____.

9. The flies and ants at the lawn party were horribly _____.

10. Leslie and Cam felt very _____ after their visiting exchange student left.

Check off these words as you use them.

adventuresome	bothersome	burdensome	flavorsome	frolicsome
lonesome	meddlesome	quarrelsome	toilsome	wholesome

SUFFIX SQUARE

_____
Name

for -**some** meaning "the same as or like something"
plus –**ness** meaning "condition or quality"

Start in the middle square with the suffixes **some** plus **ness** and combine these parts with the words in the other squares to build new words. Write each word and a definition you can think of for it in the spaces provided at the bottom of the page. Use the back of the page if you need to.

awe	lone	trouble
bother	-some + -ness	whole
meddle	fear	quarrel

_____
_____
_____
_____
_____

Copyright Dynamic Literacy LLC   www.dynamicliteracy.com

AFFIX ADDER

_____
Name

> The suffix **-some** means "the same as or like something."
>
> The suffix **–ness** means "condition or quality."

1. Write **some** and **ness** in the blank spaces after each word listed below and make a new word.
2. Tell what you think the new word means.
3. Write a sentence using the new word.

We've done one for you:

LONE means by yourself with no companion

...so LONE<u>SOME NESS</u> means <u>the condition of being without a companion.</u>

Sentence: <u>After the loss of her loved ones, her lonesomeness in an empty house was unbearable.</u>

1. TOIL means to work
   ...so TOIL _____ _____ means _____
Used in a sentence:

2. AWE means wonder and amazement
   ...so AWE_____ _____ means _____
Used in a sentence:

3. FEAR refers to being scared or afraid
   ...so FEAR _____ _____ means _____
Used in a sentence:

4. MEDDLE means to interfere with
   ...so MEDDLE _____ _____ means _____
Used in a sentence:

5. WHOLE means free of defect
   ...so WHOLE_____ _____ means _____
Used in a sentence:

6. BOTHER means to disturb
   ...so BOTHER _____ _____ means _____
Used in a sentence:

7. TIRE means to drain of energy
   ...so TIRE _____ _____ means _____
Used in a sentence:

8. ROLLICK means to behave in a carefree way
   ...so ROLLICK _____ _____ means _____
Used in a sentence:

9. QUARREL means to argue strongly and loudly
   ...so QUARREL _____ _____ means _____
Used in a sentence:

10. VENTURE means to risk danger or loss
    ...so VENTURE _____ _____ means _____
Used in a sentence:

MAGIC SQUARE

_____
Name

for -**some** meaning "the same as or like something"
plus –**ness** meaning "condition or quality"

Select the best definition for each of the words in the **some** plus **ness** family. Put the number of the definition in the proper space in the Magic Square box. If the numbers going up and down and the numbers going across all add up to the same thing, you have found the magic number!

WORDS
- A. fearsomeness
- B. adventuresomeness
- C. loathsomeness
- D. quarrelsomeness
- E. wholesomeness
- F. frolicsomeness
- G. tiresomeness
- H. toilsomeness
- I. meddlesomeness

DEFINITIONS
1. a condition of solitude
2. the quality of making you afraid
3. action that snoops into the activities of other people
4. the quality of being good for you
5. a condition requiring lots of work
6. the quality of dispute or tendency to argue
7. quality of being gross or disgusting
8. the condition of having fun
9. bravery for going into new experiences
10. conditions that make you bored

Magic Square Box

A.	B.	C.
D.	E.	F.
G.	H.	I.

Magic Number _____

Copyright Dynamic Literacy LLC   www.dynamicliteracy.com

Name _____

WORD SEARCH

Words with the suffix -some, meaning "the same as or like something"
plus -ness, meaning "quality or condition"

Find and circle all the words in the grid. Words can go across or up and down, straight or diagonally, forwards or backwards

```
F K Z X S S E N E M O S E L B U O R T K W X
X G L M S S E N E M O S E N O L K N S M R B
M W L V K H M R C F K B I T C C C S S F Y T
R H D R T R L M W P G T R R M C S R E X T F
V S D P R V L K N H F P K N X E M B N K K K
K S W I N S O M E N E S S J N N W T E B P S
F E A R S O M E N E S S O E X S C G M L F S
Q N S J M F K J D V C G M Y S M X X O S S E
B E S B F Z M Z L M R O E E B P T A S S S N
U M E S Q Z W R T H S W N R M G T G E E E E
R O N H E Z T H G E K E E V N H T S R N N M
D S E J L N H I L L M T S D S L S T U E E O
E E M J D N E O R O A M S O F E T Y T M M S
N R O N N N H M S E B D M G N K R J N O O R
S U S R Y W K E O N S E S E T Z J K E S S E
O T C K N D L R F S N O M O K K L H V H E H
M N I U R O H P L E L O M T M W X G D T L T
E E L P H Z L F S D S I M E L E L H A O D O
N V O W L V K S L E Z P O R N L N Z B O D B
E T R T R K Q J W V V C Z T L E K E X T E W
S K F P W P L A Y S O M E N E S S Q S B M R
S H Q U A R R E L S O M E N E S S S T S W T
```

adventuresomeness   irksomeness   toilsomeness

awesomeness   loathsomeness   toothsomeness

bothersomeness   lonesomeness   troublesomeness

burdensomeness   meddlesomeness   unwholesomeness

fearsomeness   playsomeness   venturesomeness

frolicsomeness   quarrelsomeness   wholesomeness

gladsomeness   tiresomeness   winsomeness

You know it!

Fill in the blanks using the words at the bottom of the page that all mean "the quality of being known by something."
Why do they mean <u>the quality of being known by something</u>?

_____

1. Ursula felt a great sense of _____ after her friends moved away.

2. The _____ of driving through the city traffic persuaded Jeff to move to the country.

3. Let's stop arguing. I'm tired of all this _____.

4. Felicia's _____ in other people's business is not appreciated.

5. The _____ of hearing Zack's same old jokes over and over is wearing us out.

6. The company advertises the _____ of the ingredients in its cereal.

7. Grandmother loved to watch the _____ of the little kittens.

8. With _____, the neighborhood kids set out to explore the orchard.

9. The _____ of the ants and bees at the barbecue drove us inside.

10. The _____ of the lions made us afraid to go near the cages.

<u>Check off these words as you use them.</u>

bothersomeness	fearsomeness	frolicsomeness	lonesomeness
meddlesomeness	quarrelsomeness	tiresomeness	troublesomeness
	venturesomeness	wholesomeness	

SUFFIX SQUARE

Name _____

for **-ity** meaning "condition or quality"

Start in the middle square with the suffix **ity** and combine this part with the words in the other squares to build new words. Write each word and a definition you can think of for it in the spaces provided at the bottom of the page. Use the back of the page if you need to.

peculiar	elastic	circular
odd	**-ity**	central
solid	complex	equal

_____

_____

_____

_____

_____

_____

Copyright Dynamic Literacy LLC   www.dynamicliteracy.com

AFFIX ADDER

_____
Name

The suffix -ity means "condition or quality."

1. Write **ity** in the blank space after each word listed below and make a new word.
2. Tell what you think the new word means.
3. Write a sentence using the new word.

We've done one for you:

   STUPID means slow to catch on or to learn

   ...so STUPID**ITY** means <u>the quality of being slow to catch on or to learn things.</u>

Sentence: <u>Be careful not to confuse ignorance with stupidity; the ignorant person may not have had a chance to learn.</u>

---

1. FORMAL means having a certain shape or style

   ...so FORMAL____ means _____

Used in a sentence:

_____

2. HUMAN means like a person

   ...so HUMAN____ means _____

Used in a sentence:

_____

3. VALID means true

   ...so VALID____ means _____

Used in a sentence:

_____

4. FAMILIAR means acquainted

   ...so FAMILIAR____ means _____

Used in a sentence:

_____

Copyright Dynamic Literacy LLC   www.dynamicliteracy.com

5. **REAL** means authentic
   ...so REAL____ means _____
Used in a sentence:

6. **SIMILAR** means like another
   ...so SIMILAR ____ means _____
Used in a sentence:

7. **ARID** means dry
   ...so ARID ____ means _____
Used in a sentence:

8. **INFERIOR** means lower, not as good
   ...so INFERIOR ____ means _____
Used in a sentence:

9. **PECULIAR** means odd or unusual
   ...so PECULIAR ____ means _____
Used in a sentence:

10. **IMMORTAL** means never going to die or be forgotten
    ...so IMMORTAL ____ means _____
Used in a sentence:

Copyright Dynamic Literacy LLC   www.dynamicliteracy.com

MAGIC SQUARE

Name _____

for -ity meaning "condition or quality"

Select the best definition for each of the words in the **ity** family. Put the number of the definition in the proper space in the Magic Square box. If the numbers going up and down and the numbers going across all add up to the same thing, you have found the magic number!

WORDS
- A. nationality
- B. uniformity
- C. vitality
- D. elasticity
- E. legality
- F. acidity
- G. oddity
- H. finality
- I. reality

DEFINITIONS
1. stiffness in manner
2. country or culture of origin
3. truth or factualness
4. point of law
5. end
6. the quality of being able to stretch or expand
7. liveliness
8. sourness
9. sameness
10. strangeness or weirdness

Magic Square Box

A.	B.	C.
D.	E.	F.
G.	H.	I.

Magic Number _____

Copyright Dynamic Literacy LLC   www.dynamicliteracy.com

Name _____

WORD SEARCH

Words with the suffix -ity, meaning "condition or quality"

Find and circle all the words in the grid. Words can go across or up and down, straight or diagonally, forwards or backwards.

```
V Y E R R Y Y T I L A R U L P X Y O
N T Q K K L T J L H R N K M V U T D
T I U V Y T I L A M R O F N I N I D
T D A B N X G M I N O R I T Y I L I
B R L X C O N F O R M I T Y M F A T
D U I R T B R Y Y J J G P B M O C Y
H S T E R L W R N T Y D M Q P R O G
L B Y N L K W Y V T I Y X E J M L G
W A Y J T A H R I N T D R L F I D Y
M L T M R W S D K I V S I O L T F T
N O L O K C I T X Y O K R U M Y Y I
B Q B N T P H E I N T M N L Q T X R
L G D I A A L W A C A I K D I I P E
K L R R L P L L B L I P R R P P L P
F X N F M I I I I L M T O O F Z X S
T L F O C T T T T N M J Y D I K Y O
T G C N Y Z Y Y T Y A V M F H R H R
R R E A L I T Y L M R N R L Q B P P
```

absurdity	liquidity	plurality
complexity	locality	priority
conformity	majority	prosperity
elasticity	minority	rapidity
equality	mobility	reality
formality	oddity	totality
informality	personality	uniformity

_____
Name

How is it?

Fill in the blanks using the words at the bottom of the page that all mean "the condition or quality of something."
Why do they mean the condition or quality of something?
_____

1. A dozen apples and twelve apples are an example of a numerical _____.

2. The _____ of a medieval castle prevented attacks from invaders.

3. Wally thought it was an _____ that he didn't have any new mail.

4. Juanita went through the _____ of shaking the queen's hand.

5. People can show their _____ by being kind to animals.

6. Edgar had worked with computers for five years, so he had a lot of _____ with them.

7. We saw a remarkable _____ in appearance between Dirk and Dee.

8. The _____ of my mother's ancestors is Swiss.

9. "That's all I'm going to say about the issue," said Raymond with _____.

10. Paula's cheerful _____ brightens everyone's day.

Check off these words as you use them.

| equality | familiarity | finality | formality | humanity |
| nationality | oddity | personality | similarity | solidity |

Copyright Dynamic Literacy LLC   www.dynamicliteracy.com

PREFIX SQUARE

_____
Name

for **pre-** meaning "at a time before" or "in front of"

Start in the middle square with the prefix **pre** and combine this part with the words in the other squares to build new words. Write each word and a definition you can think of for it in the spaces provided at the bottom of the page. Use the back of the page if you need to.

date	establish	judge
owned	**pre-**	possess
season	suppose	test

_____
_____
_____
_____
_____
_____

Copyright Dynamic Literacy LLC   www.dynamicliteracy.com

AFFIX ADDER

_____
Name

> ### The prefix **pre**- means "at a time before" or "in front of."
>
> 1. Write **pre** in the blank space in front of each word listed below and make a new word.
> 2. Tell what you think the new word means.
> 3. Write a sentence using the new word.

We've done one for you:

   VIEW means to see

   …so PRE VIEW means <u>to see at a time before.</u>

<u>Sentence</u>: Jody got to preview the movie before it was shown in theatres.
_____

1. HEAT means to warm

   …so ____ HEAT means _____

   <u>Used in a sentence</u>:
   _____

2. COOK means to make suitable for eating by applying heat

   …so ____ COOK means _____

   <u>Used in a sentence</u>:
   _____

3. COOL means to make less warm

   …so ____ COOL means _____

   <u>Used in a sentence</u>:
   _____

4. BUILT means made from parts

   …so ____ BUILT means _____

   <u>Used in a sentence</u>:
   _____

Copyright Dynamic Literacy LLC   www.dynamicliteracy.com

5. **FORM** means to shape
   ...so ____ FORM means _____
   Used in a sentence:

6. **MIX** means to combine parts
   ...so ____ MIX means _____
   Used in a sentence:

7. **PRINT** means to press letters or pictures onto a surface
   ...so ____ PRINT means _____
   Used in a sentence:

8. **SCHOOL** means a place of learning
   ...so ____ SCHOOL means _____
   Used in a sentence:

9. **SORT** means to arrange into groups
   ...so ____ SORT means _____
   Used in a sentence:

10. **TEEN** means someone between the ages of 12 and 20
    ...so ____ TEEN means _____
    Used in a sentence:

MAGIC SQUARE

_____
Name

for **pre**- meaning "at a time before" or "in front of"

Select the best definition for each of the words in the **pre** family. Put the number of the definition in the proper space in the Magic Square box. If the numbers going up and down and the numbers going across all add up to the same thing, you have found the magic number!

WORDS
A. prewarn
B. prepay
C. prefaded
D. preteen
E. pretest
F. preowned
G. preview
H. pretrial
I. predate

DEFINITIONS
1. routines that must occur before takeoff
2. to give money at a time before
3. to happen at a time before
4. a person of age less than thirteen
5. to look at ahead of time
6. a check up or examination before
7. made lighter in color at a time before
8. having been the property of another before
9. to alert before
10. the time before a court date

Magic Square Box

A.	B.	C.
D.	E.	F.
G.	H.	I.

Magic Number _____

Copyright Dynamic Literacy LLC   www.dynamicliteracy.com

WORD SEARCH

Words with the prefix pre- meaning "at a time before" or "in front of"

Find and circle all the words in the grid. Words can go across or up and down, straight or diagonally, forwards or backwards.

```
L N D D T D J P Q E L K S N C M
L R W X N S R K G G D L S P I P
P T K K Q E E D Y N X P E R R R
Q R T P D F U T L A P R S E O E
P L E A Y J Y F E R J E S S T P
R K T N E X K P E R N S O U S A
E E V R A H P S R A P C P P I C
F F P T X M E H Y E K H E P H K
L P N Q D A E R D R C O R O E A
I R K M S Z Y L P P Y O P S R G
G E T O M T I F L W K L O E P E
H C N B H U T R O S E R P K Y Q
T O X Y B P R E O W N E D H N Z
H O P E P R E C O N D I T I O N
K L R P R E M I X R M G N T K X
X P Z K J H T T S I X E E R P V
```

prearrange	preflight	prepackage
prebuild	preheat	prepossess
precondition	prehistoric	preschool
precook	prejudge	preseason
precool	premix	presort
predate	prename	presuppose
preexist	preowned	pretest

Name _____

Me First!

Fill in the blanks using the words below that all mean "at a time before" or "in front of." Why do they mean that? _____

1. It is tough being a young _____. You want to do what teenagers do.

2. Before kindergarten, I went to _____.

3. Many recipes tell you to _____ the oven so it is hot before you put the food in.

4. A morpheme you "fix" in front of a word is called a _____.

5. A word that describes a used car is _____.

6. The time of the dinosaurs is called _____ because no people lived then.

7. Practice meets for the swim team happen in the _____.

8. You can eat hot dogs right out of the package because they are _____.

9. A practice exam is also called a _____.

10. If I get to see a movie before it goes to the theaters, I get to _____ it.

Check off these words as you use them.

| prefix | pretest | prehistoric | preschool | preowned |
| precooked | preteen | preview | preheat | preseason |

SUFFIX SQUARE

_____
Name

for **-less** meaning "without; not having"

and **–ness** meaning "quality or condition"

Start in the middle square with the suffixes **less** and **ness** and combine these parts with the words in the other squares to build new words. Write each word and a definition you can think of for it in the spaces provided at the bottom of the page. Use the back of the page if you need to.

pain	help	rest
care	-less + -ness	clue
flaw	fear	harm

_____
_____
_____
_____
_____

Copyright Dynamic Literacy LLC www.dynamicliteracy.com

AFFIX ADDER

_____
Name

> The suffix **-less** means "without; not having."
>
> The suffix **–ness** means "quality or condition."

1. Write **less** and **ness** in the blank spaces after each word listed below and make a new word.
2. Tell what you think the new word means.
3. Write a sentence using the new word.

We've done one for you:

HOME means a place where one lives

...so HOME<u>LESS NESS</u> means <u>the condition of having no place to live.</u>

Sentence: People living in parks show that homelessness is a problem.

___

1. CEASE means to stop

   ...so CEASE ____ ____ means _____

   Used in a sentence:

2. EFFORT means hard work

   ...so EFFORT____ ____ means _____

   Used in a sentence:

3. FEAR refers to being scared or afraid

   ...so FEAR ____ ____ means _____

   Used in a sentence:

4. TIME refers to a period measured on the clock or calendar

   ...so TIME ____ ____ means _____

   Used in a sentence:

Copyright Dynamic Literacy LLC www.dynamicliteracy.com

5. CARE means concern
   ...so CARE____ ____ means _____
   Used in a sentence:

6. HELP means to assist
   ...so HELP ____ ____ means _____
   Used in a sentence:

7. TIRE means to drain of energy
   ...so TIRE ____ ____ means _____
   Used in a sentence:

8. LAW refers to the rules of behavior in a civilized society
   ...so LAW ____ ____ means _____
   Used in a sentence:

9. CLUE means a hint at the answer
   ...so CLUE ____ ____ means _____
   Used in a sentence:

10. JOB means a position of employment
    ...so JOB ____ ____ means _____
    Used in a sentence:

MAGIC SQUARE

_____
Name

for -**less** meaning "without; not having"
plus –**ness** meaning "quality or condition"

Select the best definition for each of the words in the **less** plus **ness** family. Put the number of the definition in the proper space in the Magic Square box. If the numbers going up and down and the numbers going across all add up to the same thing, you have found the magic number!

WORDS
A. helplessness
B. restlessness
C. lawlessness
D. carelessness
E. flawlessness
F. selflessness
G. aimlessness
H. breathlessness
I. timelessness

DEFINITIONS
1. without any degree of life
2. quality of not having the ability to relax
3. quality of not having beginning or ending
4. quality of not paying attention to important details
5. condition of being without purpose or goal
6. condition of being without mistakes
7. state of being outside what is right or fair
8. quality of having more concern for others than yourself
9. a state of being unable to do something
10. condition of being unable to breathe

Magic Square Box

A.	B.	C.
D.	E.	F.
G.	H.	I.

Magic Number _____

Copyright Dynamic Literacy LLC   www.dynamicliteracy.com

Name _____

WORD SEARCH

Words with the suffix -less, meaning "without; not having"
plus -ness, meaning "quality or condition"

Find and circle all the words in the grid. Words can go across or up and down, straight or diagonally, forwards or backwards

```
L I F E L E S S N E S S N B K N X L N L J
B L A M E L E S S N E S S D G N N L X G D
R T J K H S M R H T H Z Q P Z K V K R T S
C W Y S B E K R E E N D L E S S N E S S T
H Q R S R L S M W S N P N F Y C V Q E N S
W Y S E E F K S R X T M G M L M C N F S J
H K S N A L H R E M J L P U T Y S L E H C
W E E S T E W K F N D O E G Q S P N Z T C
C F N S H S C R N M S L B S E W S K P E T
A F S E L S N L V F E S S L S S V T A T T
R O S L E N Z F R S V E E S E N M S C R T
E R E E S E Z T S W N G E L N S E G R F Q
L T L M S S P N Y S N N M M R L S S P M R
E L E O N S E L S A S I N F E I D N S V W
S E G H E S N E H S A B H S R G A P E V Z
S S A N S M L C E F T Y S L H L B H T S B
N S T Y S P Q L S S E N S S E L K C U L S
E N N N L W E L C R E P T M L P R M K N K
S E Y E L M D W S S E N S S E L M R A H L
S S H J I X T V S L L F R R H N C Z V R T
N S D T N R N A M E L E S S N E S S R B N
```

agelessness	cluelessness	joblessness
aimlessness	effortlessness	lifelessness
blamelessness	endlessness	lucklessness
breathlessness	hairlessness	namelessness
carelessness	harmlessness	restlessness
ceaselessness	helplessness	selflessness
changelessness	homelessness	timelessness

Where is it?

Name _____

Fill in the blanks using the words at the bottom of the page that all mean "the quality of not having something."
Why do they mean <u>the quality of not having something</u>?
_____

1. Toby's _____ about his surprise birthday party was the most enjoyable part.

2. Ben did not believe in the _____ of black snakes, and so he feared them.

3. The _____ of Betsy's directions helped us find our way to her house.

4. Due to someone's _____, a fire destroyed a square mile of trees.

5. The advertised _____ of the dentist sounded good to Yvonne.

6. Sophie plays the violin with such _____ that it looks very easy.

7. The features of _____ and of belonging to no specific place make folktales interesting.

8. The _____ of the Old West ended when the marshals restored order.

9. Phil and Patricia wandered from job to job with _____ until they found something that interested them.

10. Her exhausted _____ showed that she had run hard to tell the news.

<u>Check off these words as you use them.</u>

    aimlessness   breathlessness   carelessness   cluelessness

    effortlessness   flawlessness   harmlessness   lawlessness

                            painlessness   timelessness

Copyright Dynamic Literacy LLC   www.dynamicliteracy.com

SUFFIX SQUARE

_____
Name

for -ly changed to -li meaning "like, being"

plus -ness meaning "condition or quality"

Start in the middle square with the suffix **ly** changed to **li** plus the suffix **ness** and combine these parts with the words in the other squares to build new words. Write each word and a definition you can think of for it in the spaces provided at the bottom of the page. Use the back of the page if you need to.

sick	manner	time
friend	**ly changed to li + ness**	like
home	cost	shape

_____
_____
_____
_____

Copyright Dynamic Literacy LLC   www.dynamicliteracy.com

AFFIX ADDER

_____
Name

> The suffix **-ly** means "like, being."
> The suffix **–ness** means "condition or quality."
> When **ness** is attached to a word ending with the suffix **ly**, the final **ly** is always dropped and replaced with **li.**

1. Draw a line through the final **ly** of each of the words below.
2. Write **li** and **ness** in the blank spaces after each word listed below and make a new word.
3. Tell what you think the new word means.
4. Write a sentence using the new word.

We've done one for you:
    MOTHERLY means like a female parent.
    …so MOTHER~~LY~~ _LI_ _NESS_ means _the quality of being like a female parent._
    Sentence: _With tender motherliness, the cow was licking the new-born calf._

1. SICKLY means being not well
   …so SICKLY ____ _____ means _____

2. SHAPLY means being of a certain form or outline
   …so SHAPELY ____ _____ means _____

3. MANNERLY means being of good behavior
   …so MANNERLY ____ _____ means _____

4. TIMELY means being in an expected period
   ...so TIMELY____ _____ means _____

5. EARTHLY means being of the planet where we live
   ...so EARTHLY____ _____ means _____

6. WORLDLY means being of comfort everywhere
   ...so WORLDLY____ _____ means _____

7. FRIENDLY means being someone who likes everyone
   ...so FRIENDLY____ _____ means _____

8. LOVELY means being likely to attract affection or attraction
   ...so LOVELY____ _____ means _____

9. BROTHERLY means being like a male sibling
   ...so BROTHERLY____ _____ means _____

10. SISTERLY means being like a female sibling
    ...so SISTERLY____ _____ means _____

Copyright Dynamic Literacy LLC   www.dynamicliteracy.com

MAGIC SQUARE

_____
Name

for **ly** changed to **li** meaning "like, being"
plus **ness** meaning "condition or quality"

Select the best definition for each of the words in the **ly** changed to **li** plus **ness** family. Put the number of the definition in the proper space in the Magic Square box. If the numbers going up and down and the numbers going across all add up to the same thing, you have found the magic number!

WORDS
A. princeliness
B. unmannerliness
C. untimeliness
D. grandmotherliness
E. costliness
F. shapeliness
G. manliness
H. sisterliness
I. likeliness

DEFINITIONS
1. quality of having a good chance to happen
2. quality of requiring much resources
3. quality of being like a king or queen's son
4. quality of being like a parent's mother
5. quality of not happening in a suitable period
6. quality of being like a female sibling
7. quality of not behaving well
8. quality of being like a male
9. quality of having a nice form or appearance

Magic Square Box

A.	B.	C.
D.	E.	F.
G.	H.	I.

Magic Number _____

Copyright Dynamic Literacy LLC   www.dynamicliteracy.com

WORD SEARCH

Words with suffix -ly changed to -li, meaning "like, being" plus suffix -ness, meaning "condition or quality."

Find and circle all the words in the grid. Words can go across or up and down, straight or diagonally, forwards or backwards.

```
S G T M K C Z M O T H E R L I N E S S J F
S P H R K Q S S E N I L R E T S I S L V R
E T E A C H E R L I N E S S N G B S K Y I
N C W O M A N L I N E S S Z H P L S Q M E
I H C R W D Z R R E A R T H L I N E S S N
L K C S P K W V Y T B J K N S N Z N W M D
R P K H S Y T T W H H Q K S T D N I C S L
E F X S C E M C L O R V E Q H N Z L L S I
H M A M S Z N R O P R N X O R S G N P E N
T S C T T E R I R R I L M R S B R A K N E
O H L T H G N G L L D E D E G P M M S I S
R A P V K E F I E E L E N L K L S S M L S
B P T G G V R M L I V I R J I I E D F E V
L E T F M M I L N E L O R L C N K R H K R
X L T L Q T L E I R M K L K I N E Y P I C
L I Q J N D S M E N V I L L R N W S B L K
V N K U G S P N Y N E I T B Q N E G S N L
K E G N Y G N C C M N S C L D M L S N U K
V S L M N A F T R E O Q S C K G G V S M K
L S K Q M W T F S C K R N X M R W P D R L
K J Z K F H Y S B S S E N I L E K I L Z N
```

brotherliness	loveliness	sisterliness
costliness	manliness	teacherliness
earthliness	mannerliness	timeliness
fatherliness	motherliness	unlikeliness
friendliness	orderliness	untimeliness
homeliness	shapeliness	womanliness
likeliness	sickliness	worldliness

_____
Name

Like, hey man!

Fill in the blanks using the words at the bottom of the page that all mean "quality of being like something."
Why do they mean <u>quality of being like something</u>?

_____

1. From the _____ of the secretary's desk, we guessed that he was organized.

2. With respectful _____, Jody shared her donut with her twin Lou.

3. The strange landscape had a quality of _____.

4. The restaurant manager was impressed by the _____ of the children.

5. The welcome we received and the _____ of the locals made our vacation enjoyable.

6. The _____ of paying for three telephones is too high.

7. The _____ of pears has made them a typical subject for painters.

8. We enjoyed the warmth and the _____ of the spring weather.

9. The quick _____ and fast thinking of the police officers stopped the burglary.

10. The <u>weakliness</u> of the baby hippopotamus prevented it from standing up.

<u>Check off these words as you use them.</u>

costliness	friendliness	loveliness	mannerliness	orderliness
shapeliness	sisterliness	timeliness	weakliness	worldliness

Copyright Dynamic Literacy LLC

www.dynamicliteracy.com

SUFFIX SQUARE

Name _____

for -ist meaning "an expert or a person who does, performs, or is known by"

Start in the middle square with the suffix **ist** and combine this part with the words in the other squares to build new words. Write each word and a definition you can think of for it in the spaces provided at the bottom of the page. Use the back of the page if you need to.

cartoon	art	humor
violin	-ist	solo
tour	novel	reception

_____
_____
_____
_____
_____
_____

Copyright Dynamic Literacy LLC   www.dynamicliteracy.com

AFFIX ADDER

_____
Name

> The suffix **-ist** means "an expert or a person who does, performs, or is known by."

1. Write **ist** in the blank space after each word listed below and make a new word.
2. Tell what you think the new word means.
3. Write a sentence using the new word.

We've done one for you:

   TERROR means an intense fear or threat
   ...so TERROR _IST_ means _a person who causes fear in others._

Sentence: _A terrorist doesn't care whom he or she scares._

---

1. ABSURD means making no sense
   ...so ABSURD ____ means _____
Used in a sentence:

2. BALLOON means a bag that can be filled with air
   ...so BALLOON ____ means _____
Used in a sentence:

3. COLONIAL refers to a settlement of people from a mother country
   ...so COLONIAL ____ means _____
Used in a sentence:

4. CONFORM means to be similar to or act according to a standard
   ...so CONFORM____ means _____
Used in a sentence:

5. INDIVIDUAL means one sole human being
   ...so INDIVIDUAL____ means _____
Used in a sentence:

6. LOYAL means faithful or true to another person or to one's country
   ...so LOYAL____ means _____
Used in a sentence:

7. NOVEL means a long work of fiction
   ...so NOVEL____ means _____
Used in a sentence:

8. REAL means factual and actual
   ...so REAL ____ means _____
Used in a sentence:

9. FUNDAMENTAL means basic
   ...so FUNDAMENTAL ____ means _____
Used in a sentence:

10. UNIVERSAL means belonging to everything
    ...so UNIVERSAL ____ means _____
Used in a sentence:

MAGIC SQUARE

_____
Name

for -ist meaning "an expert or a person who does, performs, or is known by"

Select the best definition for each of the words in the **ist** family. Put the number of the definition in the proper space in the Magic Square box. If the numbers going up and down and the numbers going across all add up to the same thing, you have found the magic number!

WORDS
- A. artist
- B. realist
- C. soloist
- D. alarmist
- E. centralist
- F. humorist
- G. loyalist
- H. reformist
- I. guitarist

DEFINITIONS
1. a person known for making changes for the better
2. a person who worries about everything and scares others
3. a person who performs alone
4. a person who writes or delivers jokes
5. a person known for believing only in what can be seen
6. a person known for being true to a cause
7. an expert at creating paintings or songs
8. an expert at playing a stringed instrument
9. a person who stays in the middle on most issues

Magic Square Box

A.	B.	C.
D.	E.	F.
G.	H.	I.

Magic Number _____

Copyright Dynamic Literacy LLC

WORD SEARCH

Name _____

Words that end with the suffix -ist, meaning "an expert or a person who does, performs, or is known by"

Find and circle all the words in the grid. Words can go across or up and down, straight or diagonally, forwards or backwards.

```
X K R F Z T M T D C Y J R T K A D M V
X R K E X T S E T K P Q X Y T R R H T
G F M Q C I F M S G B K R T S T J M S
P J Z B L E Y M I Z L R M N I I Y V I
W J Z A A D P N L N L T Q P R S P I L
J N Y T X L O T A F S F D F O T A O A
N O I N H V L Y I I T L M L R L N L T
L S L W E W Z O N O M S M B R T E I N
T N M L T M R O O Z N E I V E X L N E
Q Q I N P S O M L N K I D L T Z I I M
R S J L P T I T O R I J S A A J S S A
T G J Z R N S L C B Q S N T L Y T T D
J F H A M I K C A L Y G T N T I O Y N
X L C G L J O U R N A L I S T J S R U
Q R F A R D F W N G I T L L D V D T F
L R E A L I S T G K W F C G V W K C T
K D K M M M G H J T S I M R O F N O C
I L N Z N K T S I L A R U T A N W H M
K Y W B A L A R M I S T N F N X D V F
```

alarmist	finalist	novelist
artist	fundamentalist	panelist
balloonist	idealist	realist
cartoonist	journalist	receptionist
colonialist	loyalist	royalist
conformist	medalist	terrorist
defeatist	naturalist	violinist

Expert!

Name _____

Fill in the blanks using the words at the bottom of the page that all mean "an expert or person known for something."
Why do they mean <u>an expert or person known for something</u>?

_____

1. Velma is a wonderful _____ at decorating birthday cakes.

2. A _____ like Will can make a tense moment lighter with a good joke.

3. The _____ signed copies of her books at the bookstore.

4. We thought that he was a _____ because he was taking pictures of everything.

5. The _____ used both a bow and fingers to play the Hungarian melody.

6. The _____ drew a funny picture of the Senator.

7. The movie *Superman* opens with a _____ about to blow up the Eiffel Tower.

8. Nadia was a _____ who was the first ever to earn a perfect score of ten.

9. The _____ in the spelling bee had to spell one more word correctly.

10. The _____ greeted us and had us sign in at the desk and take a number.

<u>Check off these words as you use them</u>.

artist	cartoonist	finalist	humorist	medalist
novelist	receptionist	terrorist	tourist	violinist

Copyright Dynamic Literacy LLC   www.dynamicliteracy.com

SUFFIX SQUARE

Name _____

for -**ment** meaning "process, action, or result"

Start in the middle square with the suffix **ment** and combine this part with the words in the other squares to build new words. Write each word and a definition you can think of for it in the spaces provided at the bottom of the page. Use the back of the page if you need to.

accomplish	agree	pay
improve	**-ment**	entertain
appoint	assign	require

_____
_____
_____
_____
_____
_____
_____

Copyright Dynamic Literacy LLC			www.dynamicliteracy.com

AFFIX ADDER

_____
Name

> ### The suffix **-ment** means "process, action, or result"
>
> 1. Write **ment** in the blank space after each word listed below and make a new word.
> 2. Tell what you think the new word means.
> 3. Write a sentence using the new word.

We've done one for you:

   AMEND means to change by addition or deletion

   ...so AMEND<u>MENT</u> means <u>the action or result of changing by addition or deletion.</u>

<u>Sentence</u>: <u>To date there have been 27 amendments to the Constitution.</u>

1. COMMIT means to pledge
   ...so COMMIT_____ means _____
Used in a sentence:

2. ARRANGE means to place in some order
   ...so ARRANGE_____ means _____
Used in a sentence:

3. AGREE means to hold the same opinion
   ...so AGREE_____ means _____
Used in a sentence:

4. ACHIEVE means to succeed in performance
   ...so ACHIEVE_____ means _____
Used in a sentence:

Copyright Dynamic Literacy LLC   www.dynamicliteracy.com

5. **EMPLOY** means to put to use or to hire
   ...so EMPLOY_____ means _____
   Used in a sentence: _____

_____

6. **ESTABLISH** means to make firm
   ...so ESTABLISH_____ means _____
   Used in a sentence: _____

_____

7. **PLACE** means to put something
   ...so PLACE_____ means _____
   Used in a sentence: _____

_____

8. **ASSIGN** means to give work to
   ...so ASSIGN_____ means _____
   Used in a sentence: _____

_____

9. **ENJOY** means to take pleasure or satisfaction from
   ...so ENJOY_____ means _____
   Used in a sentence: _____

_____

10. **SHIP** means to send something
    ...so SHIP_____ means _____
    Used in a sentence: _____

_____

Copyright Dynamic Literacy LLC   www.dynamicliteracy.com

MAGIC SQUARE

Name _____

for -ment meaning "process, action, or result"

Select the best definition for each of the words in the **ment** family. Put the number of the definition in the proper space in the Magic Square box. If the numbers going up and down and the numbers going across all add up to the same thing, you have found the magic number!

WORDS
A. advancement
B. agreement
C. amazement
D. commandment
E. employment
F. enjoyment
G. government
H. requirement
I. statement

DEFINITIONS
1. the process of making worse
2. the process of being surprised
3. something needed
4. an order or rule that is given
5. the group that passes laws and guides the people
6. the act of liking something
7. the action of thinking the same as someone else
8. the result of being hired to work
9. the process of moving forth
10. something said or declared

Magic Square Box

A.	B.	C.
D.	E.	F.
G.	H.	I.

Magic Number _____

Copyright Dynamic Literacy LLC   www.dynamicliteracy.com

Name _____

WORD SEARCH

Words with the suffix -ment, meaning "process, action, or result"

Find and circle all the words in the grid. Words can go across or up and down, straight or diagonally, forwards or backwards.

```
Z M X A B J J R B W T D J M V Q R T T
T K Z K M T N E M E C N U O N N A N N
M N H C R A R Y Y D M M T Y T N K N E
D W E C O G Z D Y O H N T N V B Z N M
L F N M R M L E V K E R E J R Q A C E
T X C M E M M E M M F M M L N M M T G
Y N C G K G M A E E E N N Y D K E N A
D T E G B E N R N C N L T V Z P N E R
E N N M N D U A N D T T T T H Z D M U
V E J T Y S N A R N M A V J T H M N O
E M O L A A V V E R M E K K C J E G C
L E Y E L D P M C U A R N J N L N I N
O V M J A Q T J S C X Y Z T J C T S E
P E E L Y R Q E A G R E E M E N T S L
M I N W O Q M L G B Q K L M K G L A R
E H T S T E C N T N E M E V O R P M I
N C S T N E M N I A T R E T N E H M C
T A P T F T N E M H S I L B A T S E R
T H K L J H X A T T A C H M E N T L H
```

achievement	arrangement	enjoyment
advancement	assignment	entertainment
agreement	assortment	establishment
amazement	attachment	improvement
amendment	commandment	measurement
amusement	development	movement
announcement	encouragement	payment

Name _____

A Done Deal!

Fill in the blanks using the words at the bottom of the page that all mean "process, action, or result of something."

Why do they mean process, action, or result of something? _____

1. Floyd finally finished his project and was proud of his _____.

2. The _____ for the birthday party will be a movie and some games.

3. What is the age _____ to get a driver's license?

4. Redesigning the classroom brought about a major _____.

5. Willetta and Wally are in _____ about the best song of the year.

6. Jeff's _____ of riding the train for the first time was obvious on his face.

7. Dru had only one more _____ to make on the bike and it would be hers.

8. To everyone's _____, the magician pulled a rabbit out of the hat.

9. Amahl was hoping for an _____ in his job and his salary.

10. The teacher gave us a fun and exciting _____ for the day.

Check off these words as you use them.

accomplishment	advancement	agreement	amazement	assignment
enjoyment	entertainment	improvement	payment	requirement

Copyright Dynamic Literacy LLC   www.dynamicliteracy.com

SUFFIX SQUARE

Name _____

for -ion meaning "result or process"

Start in the middle square with the suffix **ion** and combine this part with the words in the other squares to build new words. Write each word and a definition you can think of for it in the spaces provided at the bottom of the page. Use the back of the page if you need to.

transcript	tract	edit
suppress	**-ion**	depress
assert	restrict	reject

_____
_____
_____
_____
_____
_____

Copyright Dynamic Literacy LLC www.dynamicliteracy.com

AFFIX ADDER

_____
Name

The suffix **-ion** means "result or process."

1. Write **ion** in the blank space after each word listed below and make a new word.
2. Tell what you think the new word means.
3. Write a sentence using the new word.

We've done one for you:

   REFLECT means to shine back
   ...so REFLECT<u>ION</u> means <u>the process of shining back.</u>

<u>Sentence</u>: <u>The reflection of the sun's rays off the mirror hurt our eyes.</u>

1. ACT means to do
   ...so ACT____ means _____
Used in a sentence:

_____

2. AFFECT means to influence
   ...so AFFECT____ means _____
Used in a sentence:

_____

3. SELECT means to choose
   ...so SELECT____ means _____
Used in a sentence:

_____

4. DEPRESS means to make lower
   ...so DEPRESS____ means _____
Used in a sentence:

_____

Copyright Dynamic Literacy LLC   www.dynamicliteracy.com

5. FORMAT means to arrange
   ...so FORMAT____ means _____
Used in a sentence:

6. IMPRESS means to affect strongly
   ...so IMPRESS____ means _____
Used in a sentence:

7. DIGEST means to absorb or take in as nutrition
   ...so DIGEST____ means _____
Used in a sentence:

8. PROCESS means to march along
   ...so PROCESS____ means _____
Used in a sentence:

9. QUEST means to seek or pursue
   ...so QUEST____ means _____
Used in a sentence:

10. COLLECT means to gather together in a group
   ...so COLLECT____ means _____
Used in a sentence:

MAGIC SQUARE

_____
Name

for -**ion** meaning "result or process"

Select the best definition for each of the words in the **ion** family. Put the number of the definition in the proper space in the Magic Square box. If the numbers going up and down and the numbers going across all add up to the same thing, you have found the magic number!

WORDS
- A. action
- B. construction
- C. correction
- D. protection
- E. eruption
- F. reflection
- G. connection
- H. election
- I. obstruction

DEFINITIONS
1. the result of blocking
2. the result of making something safe
3. the result of building something
4. the result of bursting out
5. the result of making something right
6. the result of linking together
7. the result of doing something
8. the result of choosing
9. the result of shining back

Magic Square Box

A.	B.	C.
D.	E.	F.
G.	H.	I.

Magic Number _____

Copyright Dynamic Literacy LLC

www.dynamicliteracy.com

Name _____

WORD SEARCH

Words with the suffix -ion, meaning "result or process"

Find and circle all the words in the grid. Words can go across or up and down, straight or diagonally, forwards or backwards.

```
B K K H R X V K S K K N X N Q M T N N
C M H Z O B J E C T I O N X E N O F O
T R L G N H L R N R N I V L N I R X I
Y F N L X E K O H O L T E R T R G K T
N D M K C P I H I K R C M C V D N N C
X L N T M T N T M Q T A E L T I O Q U
W D I K N W C G P I W F N R D R I Y R
T O K E Y E N M O L R Y G L M E T T T
N N V N F C O N N E C T I O N C C X S
R N O N O C P C P N J R V R P T U P N
I K I I M I O R O M O N C R P I D O I
M H Z X T Q S R E L D I G R K O O S L
J T V K R C N S R V L R T Z K N R S T
N N W N D P E M E E E M C H T P E T
Y N K H T W D F P R C N C W I R F S N
N O I T A M R O F K P T T T R V M S C
R K M Z M F K H W A Z M I I I Z N I C
H W L N O I T R E S S A I O O O L O R
N O I T C I L F F A F D Y X N N N N C
```

action	correction	invention
affection	direction	objection
affliction	election	perfection
assertion	formation	possession
collection	impression	prevention
connection	infection	production
conviction	instruction	selection

Name _____

Make It So!

Fill in the blanks using the words below that all mean "result or process of something." Why do they mean that? _____

1. Shanelle made a good _____ by dressing well.

2. Smokey the Bear is the symbol of fire _____.

3. Leaders of a democracy are chosen by voters in an _____.

4. Another word for teaching is _____.

5. A volcanic _____ spews forth lava.

6. I can seek an answer by asking a _____.

7. A parade is a _____ of people and floats.

8. Builders are involved in the _____ business.

9. Figure skaters seek _____ in their routines by scoring a 10.

10. The _____ of the sun off the water was blinding.

Check off these words as you use them

eruption	question	prevention	reflection	procession
instruction	impression	construction	perfection	election

Copyright Dynamic Literacy LLC   www.dynamicliteracy.com

SUFFIX SQUARE

_____
Name

for -ive meaning "tending or likely to"

Start in the middle square with the suffix **ive** and combine this part with the words in the other squares to build new words. Write each word and a definition you can think of for it in the spaces provided at the bottom of the page. Use the back of the page if you need to.

conduct	select	instruct
possess	-ive	restrict
protect	direct	product

_____
_____
_____
_____
_____
_____
_____

Copyright Dynamic Literacy LLC   www.dynamicliteracy.com

AFFIX ADDER

_____
Name

The suffix -ive means "tending or likely to."

1. Write **ive** in the blank space after each word listed below and make a new word.
2. Tell what you think the new word means.
3. Write a sentence using the new word.

We've done one for you:
   PREDICT means to say beforehand
   ...so PREDICT **IVE** means *tending to say beforehand.*
Sentence: *Dark clouds are often predictive of rain.*

___

1. ATTRACT means to draw toward
   ...so ATTRACT____ means _____
Used in a sentence:

2. SUPPORT means to hold up or to bear the weight of
   ...so SUPPORT____ means _____
Used in a sentence:

3. PROTECT means to shield from harm, or to guard
   ...so PROTECT____ means _____
Used in a sentence:

4. PREVENT means to keep from happening
   ...so PREVENT____ means _____
Used in a sentence:

Copyright Dynamic Literacy LLC   www.dynamicliteracy.com

5. **EXHAUST** means to tire out or use up completely
   …so EXHAUST____ means _____
Used in a sentence:

6. **DISRUPT** means to cause confusion or disorder
   …so DISRUPT____ means _____
Used in a sentence:

7. **CORRECT** means to make right
   …so CORRECT____ means _____
Used in a sentence:

8. **REFLECT** means to throw back from a surface
   …so REFLECT____ means _____
Used in a sentence:

9. **PROGRESS** means to move ahead toward a goal
   …so PROGRESS____ means _____
Used in a sentence:

10. **INFECT** means to make sick
    …so INFECT____ means _____
Used in a sentence:

MAGIC SQUARE

Name _____

for -ive meaning "tending or likely to"

Select the best definition for each of the words in the **ive** family. Put the number of the definition in the proper space in the Magic Square box. If the numbers going up and down and the numbers going across all add up to the same thing, you have found the magic number!

WORDS
A. active
B. corruptive
C. restrictive
D. massive
E. disruptive
F. effective
G. elective
H. expressive
I. sportive

DEFINITIONS
1. tending to explain clearly or to reveal
2. tending to be large in size or amount
3. likely to place limits on
4. tending to produce a desired result
5. tending to make bad or dishonest
6. tending to choose or pick out
7. tending to do things; at work
8. tending to play and have fun
9. likely to cause noise and trouble

Magic Square Box

A.	B.	C.
D.	E.	F.
G.	H.	I.

Magic Number _____

Copyright Dynamic Literacy LLC

www.dynamicliteracy.com

WORD SEARCH

Words with the suffix -ive, meaning "tending or likely to"

Find and circle all the words in the grid. Words can go across or up and down, straight or diagonally, forwards or backwards.

```
D H Y E G D C Y W I N S T R U C T I V E
Z Z R K V B I T Y L Q L M N F P D B Y E
G J M K R I K R Y E V I S S E C X E V V
T E P S E P T Z E D K L P V F P K I Q I
T V Y E B V F C N C G F I J R L S Z F T
M I Y L M D I R E R T T X M Q S F M T R
E T T E A H R T Z T C I E V E F T N N O
V C M C S C P W S E O V V R M K C W P P
I E L T S Z M R P U I R P E C B N B P P
T L Q I I C V S M T A M P W N N F O M U
C F E V V E Q C I I H K L G D S Z D S
U E V E E R L E L C N T X N N S X E I H
R R I D E P R E S S I V E E E K R Z S N
T L S K G R R N Q W R X E S G U G G R M
S R S J O Q H K T W R L S N P V R Z U J
N J E C T G K Y T K R I M T T L X D P F
O X R K P K R Z V J V Q I H B I T C T N
C Q P F G K Z M J E L V X M M X V G I L
R X X E V I T C I D E R P W W K F E V W
J R E K N R E S T R I C T I V E N T E K
```

constructive	exhaustive	predictive
corrective	expressive	protective
depressive	impressive	reflective
directive	instructive	respective
disruptive	inventive	restrictive
eruptive	massive	selective
excessive	possessive	supportive

Name _____

Maybe....

Fill in the blanks using the words below that all mean "tending to."
Why do they mean <u>tending to</u>? _____

1. A piece of metal that can draw electricity through itself is called _____.

2. I am very _____ of my little sister if someone threatens her.

3. Peanut butter must find jelly very _____; they make a good sandwich!

4. A _____ earthquake can do a lot of damage.

5. It is hard to concentrate when Thad is _____ in class.

6. It is _____ for you to only tell me part of the truth.

7. An _____ amount of noise at a party can result in a call to the police.

8. A _____ force is one which tends to take away from.

9. A _____ force is one which tends to make free from error.

10. Polished metal is a _____ surface; a brown sock is not.

<u>Check off these words as you use them</u>

massive	subtractive	protective	perfective	attractive
conductive	disruptive	reflective	deceptive	excessive

Copyright Dynamic Literacy LLC   www.dynamicliteracy.com

SUFFIX SQUARE

_____
Name

for -ive meaning "tending toward an action"

and –ly meaning "how or in what way something is done"

Start in the middle square with the suffixes **ive** and **ly** and combine these parts with the words in the other squares to build new words. Write each word and a definition you can think of for it in the spaces provided at the bottom of the page. Use the back of the page if you need to.

attract	correct	excess
suggest	-ive + -ly	select
protect	mass	instinct

_____
_____
_____
_____
_____
_____

Copyright Dynamic Literacy LLC   www.dynamicliteracy.com

AFFIX ADDER

_____
Name

> The suffix **–ive** means "tending toward."
>
> The suffix **–ly** means "how or in what way something is done."

1. Write **ive** and **ly** in the blank spaces after each word listed below and make a new word.
2. Tell what you think the new word means.
3. Write a sentence using the new word.

We've done one for you:
   PROGRESS means steps forward
   …so PROGRESS<u>IVE</u> <u>LY</u> means <u>in a manner of stepping forward.</u>

Sentence: <u>With practice, our reading became progressively better.</u>

---

1. ASSERT means to say with certainty
   …so ASSERT_____ ____ means _____

Used in a sentence:

_____

2. SELECT means to choose from a group
   …so SELECT_____ ____ means _____

Used in a sentence:

_____

3. PROTECT means to shield from harm
   …so PROTECT_____ ____ means _____

Used in a sentence:

_____

4. PRODUCT refers to the output of work
   …so PRODUCT_____ ____ means _____

Used in a sentence:

_____

Copyright Dynamic Literacy LLC   www.dynamicliteracy.com

5. POSSESS means to claim and hold as one's own
   ...so POSSESS____ ___ means _____
Used in a sentence:

6. INSTINCT refers to a behavior one is born with
   ...so INSTINCT____ ___ means _____
Used in a sentence:

7. EXCESS means in great abundance
   ...so EXCESS____ ___ means _____
Used in a sentence:

8. EXPRESS means to say
   ...so EXPRESS____ ___ means _____
Used in a sentence:

9. CORRECT means to make right
   ...so CORRECT____ ___ means _____
Used in a sentence:

10. ADOPT means to take as one's own
    ...so ADOPT____ ___ means _____
Used in a sentence:

MAGIC SQUARE

_____
Name

for **-ive** meaning "tending toward an action"
plus **-ly** meaning "how or in what way something is done"

Select the best definition for each of the words in the **ive** plus **ly** families. Put the number of the definition in the proper space in the Magic Square box. If the numbers going up and down and the numbers going across all add up to the same thing, you have found the magic number!

WORDS
A. digressively
B. predictively
C. successively
D. combatively
E. effectively
F. excessively
G. suggestively
H. sportively
I. obsessively

DEFINITIONS
1. so as to have the features of an inherited trait
2. so as to move off topic
3. so as to have extreme concern and attention
4. with good results
5. in a playful manner
6. in a manner having the features of a fight
7. so as to follow in order
8. in a manner going beyond the norm
9. in a manner that confirms what we might have thought beforehand
10. so as to bring up into the mind

Magic Square Box

A.	B.	C.
D.	E.	F.
G.	H.	I.

Magic Number _____

Copyright Dynamic Literacy LLC   www.dynamicliteracy.com

Name _____

WORD SEARCH

Words with the suffix -ive, meaning "tending or likely to" plus -ly, meaning "how or in what way something is done"

Find and circle all the words in the grid. Words can go across or up and down, straight or diagonally, forwards or backwards

```
Z P Y L E V I S S E C X E Y C W Z Q N Y R
L N R F Z Z K C B W I N T U I T I V E L Y
B Q L O D F T D Y L E V I S S E S S O P R
N N B C T N L Z I N S T I N C T I V E L Y
X J Z M A E K J Q L X L R D X G Y H D K M
Y M T Z T Y C R E A C T I V E L Y B P B Z
L R Y V T L C T T D C P J P E Y F M R Y Q
E K L J R E H Y I W M D W V K Q C Y E L C
V N E X A V M B G V Z N I T P C N L V E I
I C V N C I Y F N R E T B R P Y Y E E V N
T O I R T S D L M D C L O T L L P V N I T
C R S K I S L C E E T D Y E E K D I T T E
E R S W V E F L F V U P V V T R N T I C R
J E E T E S Q F L C I I I N J Q D C V U A
B C R N L B E Y T M T S Q K D J B E E R C
U T P R Y O P I L C S H S M M G B L L T T
S I X N L C V T E A R J F E W G W L Y S I
Y V E V M E T L M K L C B N R T V O J N V
C E Y M L X E T M X H H T N L P F C Y I E
M L K Y T S Z P W T B K K Y L W P H P W L
R Y L E V I T R E S S A G T P M N O L Z Y
```

- assertively
- attractively
- collectively
- correctively
- effectively
- excessively
- expressively
- instinctively
- instructively
- interactively
- intuitively
- massively
- obsessively
- oppressively
- possessively
- preventively
- productively
- protectively
- reactively
- selectively
- subjectively

Name _____

I'm Leaning!

Fill in the blanks using the words at the bottom of the page that all mean "so as to tend toward something."

Why do they mean <u>so as to tend toward something</u>?

_____

1. Chopin's music must be played very _____ to convey the right mood.

2. The whole class played _____ with the computer WordBuild game.

3. Mrs. Eavis always has the room decorated neatly and _____ on the first day of school.

4. The fish swam _____ back up the river to lay their eggs.

5. The weather has been _____ hot for this time of year.

6. For the fundraiser, the class _____ raised one hundred dollars.

7. "First, do no harm," the Father of Medicine said _____.

8. Ania _____ picked out all the red jelly beans from the bowl.

9. The huge canyon stretched _____ all the way to the horizon.

10. The mother duck marched her chicks _____ across the road.

<u>Check off these words as you use them</u>.

| attractively | collectively | excessively | expressively | instinctively |
| instructively | interactively | massively | protectively | selectively |

Copyright Dynamic Literacy LLC   www.dynamicliteracy.com

SUFFIX SQUARE

Name _____

for -ful meaning "having a lot of"

Start in the middle square with the suffix **ful** and combine this part with the words in the other squares to build new words. Write each word and a definition you can think of for it in the spaces provided at the bottom of the page. Use the back of the page if you need to.

delight	wonder	harm
fate	**-ful**	disgust
dread	law	forget

_____

_____

_____

_____

_____

_____

Copyright Dynamic Literacy LLC   www.dynamicliteracy.com

AFFIX ADDER

_____
Name

The suffix **-ful** means "having a lot of."

1. Write **ful** in the blank space after each word listed below and make a new word.
2. Tell what you think the new word means.
3. Write a sentence using the new word.

We've done one for you:

   CARE refers to caution
   ...so CARE_ful_ means _having a lot of caution._
Sentence: _Be careful when crossing the street._

_____

1. ART refers to beautiful creations
   ...so ART_____ means _____
Used in a sentence:

_____

2. CHEER refers to happiness
   ...so CHEER_____ means _____
Used in a sentence:

_____

3. COLOR refers to the surface appearance of a thing
   ...so COLOR_____ means _____
Used in a sentence:

_____

4. DELIGHT refers to pleasure and joy
   ...so DELIGHT_____ means _____
Used in a sentence:

_____

Copyright Dynamic Literacy LLC   www.dynamicliteracy.com

5. DISGRACE refers to shame
   ...so DISGRACE _____ means _____
   Used in a sentence:

6. RESPECT refers to honor, as for one's mother or father
   ...so RESPECT _____ means _____
   Used in a sentence:

7. FEAR refers to the feeling of fright
   ...so FEAR_____ means _____
   Used in a sentence:

8. GRACE refers to smooth behavior
   ...so GRACE _____ means _____
   Used in a sentence:

9. GLEE refers to delight
   ...so GLEE _____ means _____
   Used in a sentence:

10. HELP refers to aid
    ...so HELP_____ means _____
    Used in a sentence:

MAGIC SQUARE

_____
Name

for **-ful** meaning "having a lot of"

Select the best definition for each of the words in the suffix **ful** family. Put the number of the definition in the proper space in the Magic Square box. If the numbers going up and down and the numbers going across all add up to the same thing, you have found the magic number!

WORDS
- A. faithful
- B. painful
- C. cheerful
- D. doubtful
- E. forgetful
- F. frightful
- G. healthful
- H. mindful
- I. wasteful

DEFINITIONS
1. remembering
2. not fully believing
3. having a lot of happiness and joy
4. scary
5. causing hurt
6. tending to be good for you
7. tending to be truthful; as good as one's word
8. using up or spending unwisely
9. unable to remember

Magic Square Box

A.	B.	C.
D.	E.	F.
G.	H.	I.

Magic Number _____

Copyright Dynamic Literacy LLC   www.dynamicliteracy.com

WORD SEARCH

Words with the suffix -ful, meaning "having a lot of"

Find and circle all the words in the grid. Words can go across or up and down, straight or diagonally, forwards or backwards.

```
P D D T L U F Y A L P T X R H T
S L K W N L U F E T A H L L R
B O U F H Q B J R Y N M U H L W
C L U F E F L T Q B N F A L I F
C P C L P A K L T F T R U L N W
R R F U F L R R Q R M F L Y L R
T M R F M U E F U F E F U U X L
M R Y R X F L H U R U Y F M W U
T E P E L A G L A L Q D E N M F
Y S A T U T F C D D E D P N J R
Q T I S F E T W T E K Y O B K A
M F N A H F L N N L C M H N T E
Q U F M S U C M I N D F U L L T
R L U T I L G L E E F U L P T J
R M L M W N K M H Y F B M B N X
T A C T F U L P R L U F E K A W
```

careful	hopeful	restful
fateful	hurtful	soulful
fearful	masterful	tactful
gleeful	mindful	tearful
harmful	needful	wakeful
hateful	painful	willful
helpful	playful	wishful

Name _____

Bursting at the seams!

Fill in the blanks using the words at the bottom of the page that all mean "having a lot of something."

Why do they mean <u>having a lot of something</u>? _____

1. Jackie was so _____ to leave the groceries out in the car all day.

2. The friendly neighbors pitched in and were _____ to us on moving day.

3. If we behave in a _____ manner toward others, life goes more smoothly.

4. Roberto was not even aware that _____ thieves had taken his watch.

5. A carpet of _____ flowers sprang up after the rain.

6. Everyone had a _____ time at the party.

7. Drinking too many sodas is _____ to the teeth.

8. Getting a flu shot is _____ only for a second.

9. Turn off lights when you leave the room, so as not to be _____ of energy.

10. People who are _____ brighten the day, but grouchy people ruin it.

<u>Check off these words as you use them.</u>

| artful | cheerful | colorful | delightful | forgetful |
| harmful | helpful | painful | respectful | wasteful |

Copyright Dynamic Literacy LLC   www.dynamicliteracy.com

SUFFIX SQUARE

_____
Name

for -ful meaning "having a lot of"

plus -ness meaning "quality or condition"

Start in the middle square with the suffixes **ful** and **ness** and combine these parts with the words in the other squares to build new words. Write each word and a definition you can think of for it in the spaces provided at the bottom of the page. Use the back of the page if you need to.

force	art	care
fear	**-ful + -ness**	hope
grace	pain	truth

_____

_____

_____

_____

_____

Copyright Dynamic Literacy LLC   www.dynamicliteracy.com

AFFIX ADDER

_____
Name

> The suffix **-ful** means "having a lot of."
>
> The suffix **–ness** means "condition or quality."

1. Write **ful** and **ness** in the blank spaces after each word listed below and make a new word.
2. Tell what you think the new word means.
3. Write a sentence using the new word.

We've done one for you:
　　BOAST means to brag
　　...so BOAST<u>FUL</u> <u>NESS</u> means <u>the quality of a lot of bragging.</u>

Sentence: Tony's boastfulness after winning the game meant no one wanted to play with him again.

___

1. CHEER means happiness
　　...so CHEER____ _____ means_____
Used in a sentence:

2. WASTE means to spend or use needlessly
　　...so WASTE____ _____ means _____
Used in a sentence:

3. PEACE means a condition of security and well-being
　　...so PEACE____ _____ means _____
Used in a sentence:

4. HELP means assistance or aid
　　...so HELP____ _____ means _____
Used in a sentence:

Copyright Dynamic Literacy LLC　　　　　　　　　　　www.dynamicliteracy.com

5. FORGET means to put out of mind
   ...so FORGET____ _____ means _____
   Used in a sentence:

6. DOUBT means a lack of faith or belief
   ...so DOUBT____ _____ means _____
   Used in a sentence:

7. SKILL means a special ability
   ...so SKILL ____ _____ means _____
   Used in a sentence:

8. FRIGHT means fear
   ...so FRIGHT____ _____ means _____
   Used in a sentence:

9. THANK means to express appreciation
   ...so THANK ____ _____ means _____
   Used in a sentence:

10. TRUST means confidence
    ...so TRUST____ _____ means _____
    Used in a sentence:

MAGIC SQUARE

_____
Name

for **-ful** meaning "having a lot of" plus **–ness** meaning "quality or condition"

Select the best definition for each of the words in the **ful** plus **ness** family. Put the number of the definition in the proper space in the Magic Square box. If the numbers going up and down and the numbers going across all add up to the same thing, you have found the magic number!

WORDS
A. harmfulness
B. gracefulness
C. carefulness
D. gleefulness
E. thankfulness
F. purposefulness
G. tastefulness
H. tearfulness
I. thoughtfulness

DEFINITIONS
1. a condition tending to promote good health
2. a quality of watching out and being safe
3. condition of being about to cry
4. a condition of being happy
5. a condition of being good to eat or pleasant to see
6. quality of having an aim or goal
7. quality of being nimble and mannerly
8. personal quality of expressing appreciation
9. the quality of being able to hurt
10. a quality of consideration for others

Magic Square Box

A.	B.	C.
D.	E.	F.
G.	H.	I.

Magic Number _____

Copyright Dynamic Literacy LLC   www.dynamicliteracy.com

WORD SEARCH

Words with the suffix -ful, meaning "having a lot of" plus -ness, meaning "quality or condition"

Find and circle all the words in the grid. Words can go across or up and down, straight or diagonally, forwards or backwards

```
B M Y Y S S E N L U F G N I N A E M R D M
H E A L T H F U L N E S S M S C C H S L X
B R W H E L P F U L N E S S S M Q S R R G
S S E N L U F E T S A W E L E L E K T Q H
T V R V J Z L K W N N N H J N N Q S B L K
L H M E H M T M N L L M R K L T V K V N W
R F O G S B Y R B U R C J U U T P I D J V
X C M U B P G P F Y A N F H F J U L S M W
D J T T G M E E R R W T A Q S X R L S S X
S Q M S J H T C E T H R S Y S G P F E S V
S B Y N S A T F T G M S M X I C O U N E S
E M M S F E U F I F E P C L L C S L L N S
N N H L S L N L U N U Y P N B Q E N U L E
L P V H N E E L L L Y L N Q M J F E F U N
U L W E L D N U U J N N N M Y Y U S D F L
F W S X J E F L H F B E J E Z L L S A E U
E S N B S E N L U M N Z S G S R N V E C F
C Y Q S E G R W C F W I B S Y S E M R A D
R D Q L J R N N W F E L A H L G S M D R N
O J G H R N Y N W N Z S R P Z M S R W G I
F P J M N Q T S S E N L U F R O L O C M M
```

blissfulness	gleefulness	painfulness
carefulness	gracefulness	purposefulness
colorfulness	harmfulness	respectfulness
delightfulness	healthfulness	skillfulness
dreadfulness	helpfulness	thoughtfulness
fatefulness	meaningfulness	usefulness
forcefulness	mindfulness	wastefulness

Name _____

Seems Like ….

Fill in the blanks using the words at the bottom of the page that all mean "the quality of having a lot of something."
Why do they mean <u>the quality of having a lot of something</u>?
_____

1. With great _____, Archie placed the last block on top of the tower he had built.

2. Ted appreciated Polly's _____ of sending a card when he had his tonsils out.

3. The judge questioned the _____ of the prejudiced witnesses.

4. The swans glided across the lake with beautiful and smooth _____.

5. The _____ of the hurricane blew the boat out of the water.

6. We knew she had heard good news when she came smiling out of the meeting with such _____.

7. We can cut down on _____ of energy by turning off unused lights.

8. Evita's _____ allowed us to finish the job fast and accurately.

9. The rescued miners expressed their _____ for people's concern.

10. Morgan enjoyed the quiet and _____ of the cabin far up in the mountain.

<u>Check off these words as you use them</u>.

carefulness	cheerfulness	forcefulness	gracefulness
helpfulness	peacefulness	thankfulness	thoughtfulness
	truthfulness	wastefulness	

SUFFIX SQUARE

Name _____

for -ize meaning "to cause to become or to cause to be like"

Start in the middle square with the suffix **ize** and combine this part with the words in the other squares to build new words. Write each word and a definition you can think of for it in the spaces provided at the bottom of the page. Use the back of the page if you need to.

vital	annual	normal
popular	**-ize**	real
central	natural	magnet

_____
_____
_____
_____
_____
_____
_____

Copyright Dynamic Literacy LLC   www.dynamicliteracy.com

AFFIX ADDER

_____
Name

> The suffix **-ize** means "to cause to become or to cause to be like."

1. Write **ize** in the blank space after each word listed below and make a new word.
2. Tell what you think the new word means.
3. Write a sentence using the new word.

We've done one for you:
   RUBBER refers to elastic, waterproof material from which many things are made
   ...so RUBBER<u>IZE</u> means <u>to cause to be like rubber.</u>

Sentence: <u>You can rubberize your coat to make it waterproof.</u>

1. EQUAL means of the same number or quality
   ...so EQUAL ____ means _____
Used in a sentence:

2. FINAL means the end or limit
   ...so FINAL ____ means _____
Used in a sentence:

3. FORMAL means having a definite shape or style
   ...so FORMAL ____ means _____
Used in a sentence:

4. IDOL means an image or person that is adored
   ...so IDOL ____ means _____
Used in a sentence:

Copyright Dynamic Literacy LLC   www.dynamicliteracy.com

5. **UNIVERSAL** means belonging to everybody or to the whole world
   ...so UNIVERSAL ____ means _____
   Used in a sentence:

6. **PERSONAL** means private
   ...so PERSONAL____ means _____
   Used in a sentence:

7. **TERROR** means great fear
   ...so TERROR ____ means _____
   Used in a sentence:

8. **INTERNAL** means located within limits or borders
   ...so INTERNAL ____ means _____
   Used in a sentence:

9. **PLURAL** means more than one
   ...so PLURAL ____ means _____
   Used in a sentence:

10. **GENERAL** means overall or basic
    ...so GENERAL ____ means _____
    Used in a sentence:

MAGIC SQUARE

_____
Name

for -ize meaning "to cause to become or to cause to be like"

Select the best definition for each of the words in the **ize** family. Put the number of the definition in the proper space in the Magic Square box. If the numbers going up and down and the numbers going across all add up to the same thing, you have found the magic number!

WORDS
A. motorize
B. personalize
C. localize
D. equalize
E. modernize
F. idolize
G. visualize
H. vaporize
I. legalize

DEFINITIONS
1. to cause to become mist or tiny bits of water
2. to cause to be balanced
3. to make suitable for a specific place
4. to make into an adored hero
5. to design for a specific individual
6. to cause to be seen in the mind
7. to equip with an engine
8. to cause to be allowable or right
9. to cause to be up-do-date

Magic Square Box

A.	B.	C.
D.	E.	F.
G.	H.	I.

Magic Number _____

Copyright Dynamic Literacy LLC   www.dynamicliteracy.com

WORD SEARCH

Words with the suffix -ize, meaning "to cause to become or to cause to be like"

Find and circle all the words in the grid. Words can go across or up and down, straight or diagonally, forwards or backwards.

```
N L T L Y P K B F T E R R O R I Z E
E W H Q W Y E O E B M W L E R E L Z
V Z M F B V R R J Q M B Z K Z E G I
E C I L F M T K S O U I Z I Z M Y R
Z E Q N A M X C T O L A L I K F K O
I G Z L O J R O N A N A L H P T T H
L Z I I C R R T T B I A L I W R C T
A Z R V R I T R B T T Q L M Z N P U
E M D K Z O O A I I V V K I R E L A
D R O E K M M N P Y R A K N Z R M E
I L Y B M P I A T N K P G N F E O Z
J N N I I Q C K L L K O F B I F R I
P F W T H L L V L G M R H Z N L A L
M I N D I V I D U A L I Z E A M L A
T C O L O R I Z E R L Z R F L J I E
K M L K J T W F E N W E T T I C Z R
P M R E Z I L A R E N E G N Z X E L
P P K L E Z I L A M R O N D E T C H
```

authorize	glamorize	motorize
capitalize	idealize	normalize
colorize	immortalize	patronize
equalize	individualize	personalize
finalize	initialize	realize
formalize	mobilize	terrorize
generalize	moralize	vaporize

Name _____

Abra-Kadabra!

Fill in the blanks using the words at the bottom of the page that all mean "to cause to become something."

Why do they mean <u>to cause to become something</u>? _____

1. The candidate's enthusiastic speech served to _____ the crowd and give them hope.

2. You can _____ three elements: iron, nickel, and cobalt.

3. We kept pouring water between the glasses to _____ how much we each had.

4. The editor asked the proofreaders to _____ the copy so it could be printed.

5. Owen and Warren _____ their grandparents and love visiting with them.

6. Dr. Sagan was one of the first to _____ the study of the stars and to encourage more people to study astronomy.

7. Many people _____ their license plates with their own birthdates.

8. It is very difficult to _____ about what specific groups of people think.

9. Should you _____ the names of the days of the week?

10. Mom and Dad had to _____ and sign five places on the sales contract.

<u>Check off these words as you use them.</u>

capitalize	equalize	finalize	generalize	idolize
initialize	magnetize	personalize	popularize	vitalize

Copyright Dynamic Literacy LLC

www.dynamicliteracy.com

SUFFIX SQUARE

Name _____

for -ate meaning "to cause to become or to act on in a certain way"

Start in the middle square with the suffix **ate** and combine this part with the words in the other squares to build new words. Write each word and a definition you can think of for it in the spaces provided at the bottom of the page. Use the back of the page if you need to.

valid	hyphen	alien
pollen	**-ate**	decor
domestic	fraction	carbon

_____

_____

_____

_____

_____

_____

Copyright Dynamic Literacy LLC   www.dynamicliteracy.com

AFFIX ADDER

_____
Name

The suffix -ate means "to cause to become or to act on in a certain way."

1. Write **ate** in the blank space after each word listed below and make a new word.
2. Tell what you think the new word means.
3. Write a sentence using the new word.

We've done one for you:
   DOMESTIC means tame
   ...so DOMESTIC<u>ATE</u> means <u>to cause to become tame.</u>
Sentence: <u>It is difficult to domesticate an adult wild animal.</u>

1. HYPHEN is a mark indicating a break in a word or words
   ...so HYPHEN____ means _____
Used in a sentence:

2. ALIEN means strange
   ...so ALIEN____ means _____
Used in a sentence:

3. AUTHENTIC means genuine
   ...so AUTHENTIC____ means _____
Used in a sentence:

4. FABRIC means a physical structure
   ...so FABRIC____ means _____
Used in a sentence:

Copyright Dynamic Literacy LLC   www.dynamicliteracy.com

5. **DECOR** means a pleasing pattern or ornament
   …so DECOR____ means _____
Used in a sentence:

6. **LIQUID** means in a state able to flow
   …so LIQUID____ means _____
Used in a sentence:

7. **MARGIN** means the edge
   …so MARGIN____ means _____
Used in a sentence:

8. **ORIGIN** means the point at which something comes into being
   …so ORIGIN____ means _____
Used in a sentence:

9. **VALID** means true or strong
   …so VALID____ means _____
Used in a sentence:

10. **POLLEN** is the yellow powder in flowers
    …so POLLEN____ means _____
Used in a sentence:

MAGIC SQUARE

_____
Name

for -ate meaning "to cause to become or to act on in a certain way"

Select the best definition for each of the words in the **ate** (verb) family. Put the number of the definition in the proper space in the Magic Square box. If the numbers going up and down and the numbers going across all add up to the same thing, you have found the magic number!

WORDS
A. domesticate
B. circulate
C. locate
D. liquidate
E. impersonate
F. educate
G. decorate
H. abbreviate
I. validate

DEFINITIONS
1. to cause to be heard
2. to find the place of
3. to make shorter
4. to melt down; to turn into cash
5. to cause to be adorned or pretty
6. to cause to know something
7. to move around
8. to copy the behavior of another human
9. to make tame or comfortable with houses
10. to establish the strength or truth of

Magic Square Box

A.	B.	C.
D.	E.	F.
G.	H.	I.

Magic Number _____

Copyright Dynamic Literacy LLC

www.dynamicliteracy.com

Name _____

WORD SEARCH

Words with the suffix -ate, meaning "to cause to become or to act on in a certain way"

Find and circle all the words in the grid. Words can go across or up and down, straight or diagonally, forwards or backwards.

```
D M P O L L I N A T E T Y P K L N K W L
F A N T A S T I C A T E E N F D L X X Q
E P G I E T A R O C E D Z M N T E Y L M
T T K N K D R F K D E M M J E T Q J Y T
A W Y V Q B M R B Y N T R K A N M L R K
N E T A N I S S A S S A A N M N D M L T
O T P L Y R K H Q K D L E G G H L A R P
S A Z I T F Q L Y O R I G I N A T E T E
R D E D L R C E M P L B P L E O M D T E
E I T A R A M E T A H G R T M X L A H E
P U A T P C S F N A N E A Q J M C O T J
M Q D E P T V Q X N N M N Q C I B A R H
I I I R I I M F A B R I C A T E L Q Y P
G L L C D O N B F O P L U N T U M R D W
Q M A X M N P L F K L G E R C E T F Z R
K T V G T A W N L W L H J R R L I Z H C
E H Z R C T R G Y F T V I F F X R Y Q B
Y Y Y P W E M Q F U D C V V A K G V D H
K X N X T N P C A V L K Z T J L D Y Z M
F V Y K Z D F H W C W N E K D L V H N Q
```

alienate	fabricate	invalidate
assassinate	fantasticate	liquidate
authenticate	fixate	originate
circulate	formate	pollinate
decorate	fractionate	prolongate
domesticate	hyphenate	ruinate
emendate	impersonate	validate

Name: _____

Maybe....

Fill in the blanks using the words below that all mean "to cause to become or to act on in a certain way."

Why do they mean <u>to cause to become or to act on in a certain way</u>?

_____

1. Zoe managed to _____ everyone with her strange behavior.

2. Bees _____ flowers.

3. A high score on a test helps you _____ the strength of your knowledge.

4. Sally tried to _____ her older sister to get into the movie.

5. Ms. Reeves decides to _____ her classroom with word walls.

6. Sometimes people with two last names _____ them.

7. You can _____ orange juice to make orange soda!

8. Most people _____ the phrase **post meridiem** to **p.m**.

9. It can be very hard to _____ a wild animal.

10. Scientists try to answer questions like "Where did life on earth _____?"

<u>Check off these words as you use them.</u>

| decorate | abbreviate | pollinate | originate | hyphenate |
| impersonate | validate | domesticate | alienate | carbonate |

SUFFIX SQUARE

_____
Name

for **-ous** meaning "full of or being like something"

Start in the middle square with the suffix **ous** and combine this part with the words in the other squares to build new words. Write each word and a definition you can think of for it in the spaces provided at the bottom of the page. Use the back of the page if you need to.

riot	cancer	venom
valor	**-ous**	ruin
pomp	traitor	treason

_____
_____
_____
_____
_____
_____

Copyright Dynamic Literacy LLC   www.dynamicliteracy.com

AFFIX ADDER

_____
Name

> The suffix **-ous** means "full of or being like something."
>
> 1. Write **ous** in the blank space after each word listed below and make a new word.
> 2. Tell what you think the new word means.
> 3. Write a sentence using the new word.

We've done one for you:

 OUTRAGE refers to an act that is extreme or offensive

 ...so OUTRAGE <u>ous</u> means like something with extreme qualities.

Sentence: The behavior of a few citizens is outrageous.

---

1. CANCER means a mass of harmful tissue in the body

   ...so CANCER ____ means _____.

   Used in a sentence:

   _____

2. HUMOR means a comic or amusing quality

   ...so HUMOR ____ means _____

   Used in a sentence:

   _____

3. JOY means pleasurable feeling

   ...so JOY ____ means _____

   Used in a sentence:

   _____

4. ODOR means smell

   ...so ODOR ____ means _____

   Used in a sentence:

   _____

Copyright Dynamic Literacy LLC   www.dynamicliteracy.com

5. PROSPER means to succeed or do well
   ...so PROSPER ____ means _____
Used in a sentence:

6. RIOT means disturbance and noise
   ...so RIOT ____ means _____
Used in a sentence:

7. SLUMBER means sleep
   ...so SLUMBER ____ means _____
Used in a sentence:

8. SPLENDOR means brightness or brilliance
   ...so SPLENDOR ____ means _____
Used in a sentence:

9. TREASON means betrayal of one's country
   ...so TREASON ____ means _____
Used in a sentence:

10. MOMENT means a particular time, of some importance
    ...so MOMENT ____ means _____
Used in a sentence:

MAGIC SQUARE

_____
Name

for -ous meaning "full of or being like something"

Select the best definition for each of the words in the **ous** family. Put the number of the definition in the proper space in the Magic Square box. If the numbers going up and down and the numbers going across all add up to the same thing, you have found the magic number!

WORDS
- A. humorous
- B. joyous
- C. odorous
- D. vigorous
- E. prosperous
- F. thunderous
- G. slumberous
- H. scandalous
- I. vaporous

DEFINITIONS
1. having the qualities of beauty
2. full of happiness
3. having the quality of gas
4. full of life and energy
5. full of sleepiness
6. having the quality of financial success
7. full of smelliness
8. having the quality of being very loud
9. having the quality of being funny
10. full of shock and disgrace

Magic Square Box

A.	B.	C.
D.	E.	F.
G.	H.	I.

Magic Number _____

Copyright Dynamic Literacy LLC   www.dynamicliteracy.com

174

Name _____

WORD SEARCH

Words with the suffix -ous, meaning "full of or being like something"

Find and circle all the words in the grid. Words can go across or up and down, straight or diagonally, forwards or backwards.

```
S U O R O G I V S R I O T O U S S B
X R X L L Z J U S T J Q L M X N U L
T Y H N D L O U R S L F W O R Z O P
L M P K F R O E O U M T W M K N R S
T C C R O R A D L O B Z Y E M M O C
F K T M O S O S K P L K J N H T T A
N N A P O R U U S L C P T T W W I N
P L A N O O R O H U M O R O U S A D
C V O U N T L R S P O T N U B T R A
M U S I G N D E M U X R C S D H T L
S R S R B W P C L R O N E K L H C O
M E T K W L N N P J U R P P Z M F U
R J G J M T Z A K R O I E X S L T S
B R X Q Q P B C L M P Y N D Y O W Q
M S U O R E D N O P B K O O N K R J
T S U O R O D N E L P S T U U U H P
T S L U M B E R O U S F P N S S H N
T K N T H S U O E G A R T U O X K T
```

cancerous	ponderous	slumberous
clamorous	prosperous	splendorous
humorous	pulpous	thunderous
joyous	resinous	traitorous
momentous	riotous	treasonous
odorous	ruinous	vaporous
outrageous	scandalous	vigorous

_____
Name

FULL OF IT!

Fill in the blanks using the words below that all mean "full of or being like something."

Why do they mean <u>full of or being something</u>? _____

1. Flashing, _____ clouds appeared on the horizon, so we ran home.

2. For _____ conduct in saving fellow citizens, Peggy won a medal.

3. With a good diet and _____ exercise people can stay healthy longer.

4. Reba was relieved to learn that the white spot on her skin was not _____.

5. The reunion was a _____ occasion as many had not seen each other in years.

6. The silly comment by the leader provoked _____ laughter from the audience.

7. The _____ spy was hanged for giving away military secrets.

8. Buddy felt creepy as he looked at the _____ snakes in the zoo.

9. As a rule, people spend more money as they become more _____.

10. The _____ jokes that Carlos told made everyone feel at ease.

<u>Check off these words as you use them</u>.

| cancerous | humorous | joyous | prosperous | riotous |
| thunderous | treasonous | valorous | venomous | vigorous |

PREFIX SQUARE

_____
Name

for **pro**- meaning "for or forward"

Start in the middle square with the prefix **pro** and combine this part with the words in the other squares to build new words. Write each word and a definition you can think of for it in the spaces provided at the bottom of the page. Use the back of the page if you need to.

noun	active	long
claim	**pro-**	motion
tract	pose	log

_____
_____
_____
_____
_____
_____

Copyright Dynamic Literacy LLC   www.dynamicliteracy.com

AFFIX ADDER

_____
Name

The prefix **pro-** means "for or forward."

1. Write **pro** in the blank space in front of each word listed below and make a new word.
2. Tell what you think the new word means.
3. Write a sentence using the new word.

We've done one for you:

   VISION means seeing

   ...so PROVISION means <u>seeing forward or ahead.</u>

Sentence: <u>We made provision for our camping trip by packing bottled water.</u>

1. ACTIVE means doing something
   ...so ____ ACTIVE means _____
Used in a sentence:

2. FESS means to admit or speak something
   ...so ____ FESS means _____
Used in a sentence:

3. LOG means words spoken or written
   ...so ____ LOG means _____
Used in a sentence:

4. LONG means extended; not short
   ...so ____ LONG means _____
Used in a sentence:

Copyright Dynamic Literacy LLC   www.dynamicliteracy.com

5. MOTION means movement
   ...so ____ MOTION means _____
Used in a sentence:

6. NOUN means a word designating a person, place, or thing
   ...so ____ NOUN means _____
Used in a sentence:

7. POSE means to put facts or ideas into words
   ...so ____ POSE means _____
Used in a sentence:

8. SCRIBE means to put down in writing
   ...so ____ SCRIBE means _____
Used in a sentence:

9. TRACT means an old-fashioned expression for a stretch of time
   ...so ____ TRACT means _____
Used in a sentence:

10. CLAIM means to announce or declare
    ...so ____ CLAIM means _____
Used in a sentence:

MAGIC SQUARE

_____
Name

for **pro**- meaning "for or forward"

Select the best definition for each of the words in the **pro** family. Put the number of the definition in the proper space in the Magic Square box. If the numbers going up and down and the numbers going across all add up to the same thing, you have found the magic number!

WORDS
A. proactive
B. profile
C. proclaim
D. pronoun
E. prolong
F. promotion
G. prolabor
H. propose
I. prowar

DEFINITIONS
1. for or in favor of fighting
2. a word used for a noun
3. to sort out as being part of a group and not an individual
4. to drag forward in time
5. to speak out boldly
6. serving to be for the working force
7. serving to get something done
8. to put forward an idea
9. the act of moving ahead in rank or grade

Magic Square Box

A.	B.	C.
D.	E.	F.
G.	H.	I.

Magic Number _____

Copyright Dynamic Literacy LLC   www.dynamicliteracy.com

WORD SEARCH

Words with the prefix pro- meaning "for or forward"

Find and circle all the words in the grid. Words can go across or up and down, straight or diagonally, forwards or backwards.

```
R O T C E P S O R P E K O V O R P
C Q D W E L L K N R H D N B Z K P
T D L V V Z R H H O M T I T K T T
L K R K I P R X P L R T K V G D B
W V P F T R O P R O J E C T O R T
N F Y G C O T M O N L X V L P R E
D T N R A S C C V G L C Z R D C P
R E H N O P E D I I K L O E N P E
P P T R R E T Q D N Y V K U R C F
R N R O P C O P E G I O O O U M L
O U Q O M T R X R S V N M D H L Y
T O N V L O P T I O O O O J Q B Q
R N V B L O R O R R T R Z K F W P
A O Q P K T N P P E P E C K Q G W
C R Q J C D H G Z X L L C F C J K
T P R M Q P R O P O S E B T D V R
Y W X G N O I T O M O R P D N K M
```

proactive	promotion	protector
produce	pronoun	protract
projector	pronounce	provide
prolong	propose	provider
prolonging	prospect	provision
promote	prospector	provoke
promoted	protect	provoked

Name _____

All for it!

Fill in the blanks using the words below that all mean "to do something for or forward."

Why do they mean <u>to do something for or forward</u>? _____

1. A word like *he* or *she*, used for a noun, is called a _____.

2. Having good foresight, grandmother made _____ for us cousins.

3. The _____ political party persuaded the president to attack the fort.

4. I heard the guard _____ that the Queen was about to appear.

5. We hoped that the talkative Mr. Barry would not _____ the boring meeting.

6. What solutions can you _____ for the problem?

7. What did you do to _____ the cat to scratch you?

8. The _____ person gets things done quickly that need to be done.

9. Tilly and Wanda _____ to be experts at handling kids who bully.

10. After she had worked at the store for a month, Jeanie got a _____.

<u>Check off these words as you use them</u>.

proactive	proclaim	profess	prolong	promotion
pronoun	propose	provision	provoke	prowar

Copyright Dynamic Literacy LLC   www.dynamicliteracy.com

SUFFIX SQUARE

Name _____

for -ic meaning "like or similar to"

Start in the middle square with the suffix **ic** and combine this part with the words in the other squares to build new words. Write each word and a definition you can think of for it in the spaces provided at the bottom of the page. Use the back of the page if you need to.

alphabet	hero	idiot
photograph	**-ic**	diplomat
artist	robot	myth

_____

_____

_____

_____

_____

_____

Copyright Dynamic Literacy LLC   www.dynamicliteracy.com

AFFIX ADDER

_____
Name

The suffix -**ic** means "like or similar to."

1. Write **ic** in the blank space after each word listed below and make a new word.
2. Tell what you think the new word means.
3. Write a sentence using the new word.

We've done one for you:

FORMULA means an accepted and usual way of doing something.

...so FORMULA**ic** means <u>done in a way similar to the accepted and usual way of doing that.</u>

<u>Sentence:</u> Good writers try to be creative and to avoid formulaic patterns.

---

1. ANGEL means a kind and lovable person or spirit
   ...so ANGEL____ means _____
   <u>Used in a sentence:</u>

2. DIPLOMAT means one who is skilled at dealing with others
   ...so DIPLOMAT ____ means _____
   <u>Used in a sentence:</u>

3. HERO means a person known for bravery
   ...so HERO____ means _____
   <u>Used in a sentence:</u>

4. MYTH means a story made up to illustrate certain values
   ...so MYTH____ means _____
   <u>Used in a sentence:</u>

Copyright Dynamic Literacy LLC   www.dynamicliteracy.com

5. PATRIOT means a person who loves and defends the nation
   ...so PATRIOT____ means _____
Used in a sentence:

6. OCEAN means a great body of salt water
   ...so OCEAN____ means _____
Used in a sentence:

7. SYSTEM means a group of things working together as a whole
   ...so SYSTEM____ means _____
Used in a sentence:

8. ROBOT means a machine or device that operates remotely
   ...so ROBOT____ means _____
Used in a sentence:

9. ECHO means sound reflected off a surface
   ...so ECHO____ means _____
Used in a sentence:

10. DIALECT means a pattern of speech
    ...so DIALECT____ means _____
Used in a sentence:

MAGIC SQUARE

Name _____

for -ic meaning "like or similar to"

Select the best definition for each of the words in the **ic** family. Put the number of the definition in the proper space in the Magic Square box. If the numbers going up and down and the numbers going across all add up to the same thing, you have found the magic number!

WORDS
A. heroic
B. diplomatic
C. rhythmic
D. prophetic
E. photographic
F. patriotic
G. materialistic
H. artistic
I. robotic

DEFINITIONS
1. like something very basic and simple
2. like a brave and courageous person
3. like a mechanical human
4. related to a picture taken with a camera
5. like someone who creates beautiful or clever things
6. foretelling what is to come
7. like patterns in music or poetry
8. loyal to one's fatherland
9. with tact and consideration
10. similar to someone who likes to own things

Magic Square Box

A.	B.	C.
D.	E.	F.
G.	H.	I.

Magic Number _____

Copyright Dynamic Literacy LLC   www.dynamicliteracy.com

Name _____

WORD SEARCH

Words that end with the suffix -ic, meaning "like or similar to"

Find and circle all the words in the grid. Words can go across or up and down, straight or diagonally, forwards or backwards.

```
C B K R L G E B C O J R J N B M C O
I F N G M C B C X I R A T M Q K C N
H G N M H K R G I B T G N W T E L N
P T C O D P C K C O D O A G A B D W
A T I R I A F T I G R F B N E C J P
R C T A P T Y N D K P E I O I L F C
G Q S L L R M K I N H C H M R C I K
O P I I O I C C C M M Y H L L H K C
N M L S M O D I A D N T F L C F I D
O N A T A T G T D W Y Q L R N L K V
H X E I T I X O P H C L A R O V W B
P Q D C I C P I R W T N T H T N R B
F N I H C D K D Z Q O T O L M Y L W
C I T C E L A I D M H C M Y T H I C
C A R T I S T I C M L M D G M B B K
F J Q Y M V C N X A L T M K B C X B
C I T E H P O R P P B X B Q J M N N
Q N N V W K A L P H A B E T I C F L
```

acidic	echoic	oceanic
alcoholic	heroic	organic
alphabetic	idealistic	patriotic
angelic	idiotic	phonographic
artistic	monarchic	prophetic
dialectic	moralistic	rhythmic
diplomatic	mythic	robotic

Name _____

LIKE!

Fill in the blanks using the words below that all mean "like or similar to something."

Why do they mean <u>like or similar to something</u>? _____

1. The _____ reaction of the firefighters and security guards saved many lives.

2. The Iowa cornfields stretched to the horizon and seemed _____ in size.

3. Jude has a _____ memory. She can picture things perfectly in her mind.

4. Leticia could not stand the _____ taste of the nasty cold medicine.

5. Marty's _____ talents include painting, sculpture, and violin.

6. Dragons, trolls, and other _____ characters represent the dark side of life.

7. The _____ crowd stood and sang the national anthem before the game.

8. With their jerky, _____ movements, the band was named The Droids.

9. So that the teacher could learn our names, we sat in _____ order.

10. The ambassadors used their best _____ manners and tact at the conference.

<u>Check off these words as you use them.</u>

| acidic | alphabetic | artistic | diplomatic | heroic |
| mythic | oceanic | patriotic | photographic | robotic |

Copyright Dynamic Literacy LLC   www.dynamicliteracy.com

PREFIX SQUARE

Name _____

for **con**- meaning "together, with"

Start in the middle square with the prefix **con** and combine this part with the words in the other squares to build new words. Write each word and a definition you can think of for it in the spaces provided at the bottom of the page. Use the back of the page if you need to.

join	form	duct
sequence	**con-**	tour
fluent	firm	current

_____
_____
_____
_____
_____
_____

Copyright Dynamic Literacy LLC   www.dynamicliteracy.com

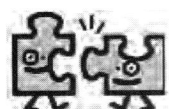

AFFIX ADDER

Name _____

The prefix **con-** means "together, with"

1. Write **con** in the blank space in front of each word listed below and make a new word.
2. Tell what you think the new word means.
3. Write a sentence using the new word.

We've done one for you:

   GENIAL means pleasant and kind

   ...so <u>CON</u>GENIAL means <u>pleasant and kind with others.</u>

Sentence: People at the party were very congenial, enjoying the same tastes and interests.

---

1. CURRENT means a steady movement

    ...so ____ CURRENT means _____

Used in a sentence:

_____

2. DUCT means something leading

    ...so ____ DUCT means _____

Used in a sentence:

_____

3. FIRM means to make solid

    ...so ____ FIRM means _____

Used in a sentence:

_____

4. FLUENT means flowing smoothly and easily

    ...so ____ FLUENT means _____

Used in a sentence:

_____

Copyright Dynamic Literacy LLC   www.dynamicliteracy.com

5. FORM means to shape
   ...so ____ FORM means _____
Used in a sentence:

6. FUSE means to mix
   ...so ____ FUSE means _____
Used in a sentence:

7. JOIN means to unite
   ...so ____ JOIN means _____
Used in a sentence:

8. SEQUENCE means a following of one thing after another
   ...so ____ SEQUENCE means _____
Used in a sentence:

9. TACT means touch
   ...so ____ TACT means _____
Used in a sentence:

10. TEXT means something woven together
    ...so ____ TEXT means _____
Used in a sentence:

MAGIC SQUARE

_____
Name

for **con**- meaning "together, with"

Select the best definition for each of the words in the **con** family. Put the number of the definition in the proper space in the Magic Square box. If the numbers going up and down and the numbers going across all add up to the same thing, you have found the magic number!

WORDS
A. configure
B. confluent
C. contacts
D. conforms
E. confronts
F. confirms
G. conducts
H. conjunctions
I. concurrent

DEFINITIONS
1. happening at the same time as something else
2. comes face to face with
3. to shape in a certain way with a certain purpose in mind
4. becomes the same pattern with
5. gets in touch together; sends a message
6. places where things join together
7. flowing together into one
8. leads together
9. proves to agree strongly with the facts

Magic Square Box

A.	B.	C.
D.	E.	F.
G.	H.	I.

Magic Number _____

Copyright Dynamic Literacy LLC   www.dynamicliteracy.com

Name _____

WORD SEARCH

Words with the prefix con- meaning "together, with"

Find and circle all the words in the grid. Words can go across or up and down, straight or diagonally, forwards or backwards.

```
Q P K C M C M K M N E F R K E M G
B B N L O K O N N S Q R L V J D N
R T T Q N K N U Z P N R F T M O
P B C V E G C F F Y L E N C Q C I
M C E U X C N U N O S T O L Y X T
K O T V R O N J R N U N L R M L A
C N A N C T T E O R J N C H C K S
O C R N Q M S C U O E K D O T S N
N L E M E R C N I Q M N N J E G E
F U D E S O O N O W E T T F R F D
R D E S R F N M T C A S N D N K N
O E F N E N D J Y C T O N J K Q O
N D N E V O U F T Q C X W O R T C
T R O D N C C C O N F I R M C L K
M N C N O J T H C O N F L U E N T
W Y N O C Q E S R U O C N O C D J
T K R C M H T S E U Q N O C V H B
```

conclude	confess	conjoin
concourse	confirm	conquest
concurrent	confluent	consequence
condensation	conform	conserve
condense	confound	construct
conduct	confront	contact
confederate	confuse	converse

Name _____

COME TOGETHER!

Fill in the blanks using the words below that all mean "to do something together or with."

Why do they mean to do something together or with? _____

1. When pieces of meaning are put together, the resulting _____ is a word.

2. On a warm day, water will _____ on the outside of a cold glass.

3. Sara said she would _____ the date of her dental appointment to make sure.

4. Lenny was not afraid to _____ the people making false accusations.

5. Mr. Casey was careful not to _____ his students with all the new facts.

6. As a _____ of the earth going around the sun, we get a year older.

7. During the storm we lost all _____ with the outside world.

8. Fred and Frieda love to watch Mr. Thomas _____ the school orchestra.

9. If you choose not to _____ to the rules, you will not be welcome anymore.

10. What town is located at the _____ of the Ohio and Mississippi Rivers?

Check off these words as you use them.

condense	conduct	confirm	conform	confront
confuse	conjunction	consequence	construction	contact

Copyright Dynamic Literacy LLC

www.dynamicliteracy.com

PREFIX SQUARE

_____
Name

for **con**- meaning "together or with"

The prefix **con** is also sometimes spelled **com**, **co**, **cor**, or **col**, depending on the first letter of the word to which it is attached. Start in the middle square with the prefix **con**- (or one of its assimilated forms) and combine this part with the words in the other squares to build new words. Write each word and a definition you can think of for it in the spaces provided at the bottom of the page. Use the back of the page if you need to.

operate	mission	league
verse	con-, co-, col-, com-, cor-	respond
motion	pact	chairman

_____

_____

_____

_____

_____

Copyright Dynamic Literacy LLC   www.dynamicliteracy.com

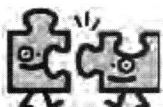

AFFIX ADDER

_____
Name

> The prefix **con-** means "together or with" and is sometimes spelled **com**, **co**, **cor**, or **col**, depending on the first letter of the word to which it is attached.

1. Write **con** or one of its alternative spellings in the blank space in front of each word listed below and make a new word.
2. Tell what you think the new word means.
3. Write a sentence using the new word.

We've done one for you:
   LAPSE means to fall or cave in
   ...so COLLAPSE means to fall downward or together in a mass.

Note that **col** is the preferred spelling of **con** because it is easier to pronounce when it attaches to the first letter of "lapse."

Sentence: I was so tired I feared I might collapse.

1. MOTION means movement
   ...so _____MOTION means _____
   Used in a sentence:

2. PACT means an agreement
   ...so _____PACT means _____
   Used in a sentence:

3. PASSION means powerful feeling
   ...so _____PASSION means _____
   Used in a sentence:

4. PATRIOT means one who loves his fatherland
   ...so _____PATRIOT means _____
   Used in a sentence:

Copyright Dynamic Literacy LLC   www.dynamicliteracy.com

5. MINGLE means to mix
   ...so _____MINGLE means _____
Used in a sentence:

6. LINEAR means straight
   ...so _____LINEAR means _____
Used in a sentence:

7. LATERAL means to the side
   ...so _____LATERAL means _____
Used in a sentence:

8. LOCATE means to place
   ...so _____LOCATE means _____
Used in a sentence:

9. RELATE means to interact or connect
   ...so _____RELATE means _____
Used in a sentence:

10. RESPOND means to answer or reply
    ...so _____RESPOND means _____
Used in a sentence:

MAGIC SQUARE

_____
Name

for con- meaning "together or with"

The prefix **con** is also sometimes spelled **com, co, cor,** or **col**, depending on the first letter of the word to which it is attached. Select the best definition for each of the words in the **con** family. Put the number of the definition in the proper space in the Magic Square box. If the numbers going up and down and the numbers going across all add up to the same thing, you have found the magic number!

WORDS
A. coworker
B. correlate
C. compassion
D. coeducation
E. correspond
F. costar
G. compress
H. cooperate
I. collinear

DEFINITIONS
1. one who shares the benefits of a will
2. the act of feeling another person's pain
3. to push together with force
4. to write back and forth with another person
5. to work with others
6. to be a top performer along with someone else
7. a partner with you at your job
8. the practice of teaching males and females together
9. to match up with
10. being in a straight line with something else

Magic Square Box

A.	B.	C.
D.	E.	F.
G.	H.	I.

Magic Number _____

Copyright Dynamic Literacy LLC   www.dynamicliteracy.com

Name _____

WORD SEARCH

Words with the prefix con- or one of its assimilated forms meaning "together or with"

Find and circle all the words in the grid. Words can go across or up and down, straight or diagonally, forwards or backwards.

```
W Y C O M M I S S I O N P G S H Z
C O E D U C A T I O N K L F S F C
K C O O P E R A T E C F Q J E T O
R N K T R W D L C C F R M Z R R M
G O C W O M Y N D O A X L M P N M
R I O N S R V K O T M P M X M B O
F T N H N O R L S P C M M V O J T
J I T W O F Q O X R S O I O C W I
P S A G P N C N R E N E M N C T O
Z O C V S O R R T N L R R M G Q N
L P T N O C C A C I R M B R I L N
T M R L C O L O P R Y Z N T O T E
R O C R L E N M T M J R T Q V C M
D C B L R D O N K V K R C B P R N
T X A R U C K L R E K R O W O C J
T T O C R K E U G A E L L O C H J
E C T D L T N O I S S A P M O C R
```

coeducation	compact	contact
collate	compassion	cooperate
colleague	compile	correlate
commingle	composition	correspond
commission	compress	cosponsor
commit	conduct	costar
commotion	conform	coworker

Name _____

Are you with it?

Fill in the blanks using the words at the bottom of the page that all mean "together or with something"

Why do they mean <u>together or something</u>? _____

1. We learn that if we _____, we get things done better and faster.

2. Carla was a _____ of mine when I worked at the book store.

3. Yves and Yvette used to _____ with each other by mail every September.

4. We wondered what all the _____ out in the hall was about.

5. If all the boxes are _____, we can carry out all the stuff in three trips.

6. Denny and Denise will _____ together in the school play.

7. New York City and Madrid are on the same line of latitude. They are _____.

8. Good reading ability will _____ with your knowledge of word parts.

9. After an awkward ten minutes, the guests began to _____ and get to know each other.

10. Greta felt _____ for the victims of the heat wave.

<u>Check off these words as you use them</u>.

| colleague | collinear | commingle | commotion | compact |
| compassion | cooperate | correlate | correspond | costar |

Copyright Dynamic Literacy LLC   www.dynamicliteracy.com

PREFIX SQUARE

_____
Name

for **ad**- meaning "to or toward"

The prefix **ad** is also sometimes spelled **a**, **ac**, **af**, **ag**, **al**, **an**, **ap**, **ar**, **as**, or **at**, depending on the first letter of the word to which it is attached. Start in the middle square with the prefix **ad** (or one of its assimilated forms) and combine this part with the words in the other squares to build new words. Write each word and a definition you can think of for it in the spaces provided at the bottom of the page. Use the back of the page if you need to.

just	claim	firm
locate	**a-, ac-, ad-, af-, ag-, al-, an-, ap-, ar-, as-, at-**	mass
point	range	tend

_____
_____
_____
_____
_____

Copyright Dynamic Literacy LLC www.dynamicliteracy.com

AFFIX ADDER

_____
Name

> The prefix **ad-** means "to or toward" and is sometimes spelled **a, ac, af, ag, al, an, ap, ar, as,** or **at**, depending on the first letter of the word to which it is attached.
>
> 1. Write **ad** or one of its alternative spellings in the blank space in front of each word listed below and make a new word.
> 2. Tell what you think the new word means.
> 3. Write a sentence using the new word.

We've done one for you:
   RANGE means to organize into an order
   ...so _AR_RANGE means _to put into order_.

Note that **ar** is the preferred spelling of **ad** because it is easier to pronounce when it attaches to the first letter of "range."

Sentence: _I needed to arrange things on my desk before beginning my work._

1. CLAIM means to demand or call out for
   ...so ____CLAIM means _____
Used in a sentence: _____

2. FIX means to place or put in stable form
   ...so ____FIX means _____
Used in a sentence: _____

3. LOCATE means to place
   ...so ____LOCATE means _____
Used in a sentence: _____

4. POINT means to direct or aim
   ...so ____POINT means _____
Used in a sentence: _____

Copyright Dynamic Literacy LLC   www.dynamicliteracy.com

5. SORT means to arrange according to kind
   ...so ____SORT means _____
Used in a sentence:

6. MASS means to assemble
   ...so ____MASS means _____
Used in a sentence:

7. GRIEVE means to experience sadness
   ...so ____GRIEVE means _____
Used in a sentence:

8. TUNE means to adjust
   ...so ____TUNE means _____
Used in a sentence:

9. NOTATE means to make notes about
   ...so ____NOTATE means _____
Used in a sentence:

10. MINISTER means to care for
    ...so ____MINISTER means _____
Used in a sentence:

Copyright Dynamic Literacy LLC   www.dynamicliteracy.com

MAGIC SQUARE

_____
Name

for **ad**- meaning "to or toward"

The prefix **ad** is also sometimes spelled **a**, **ac**, **af**, **ag**, **al**, **an**, **ap**, **ar**, **as**, or **at**, depending on the first letter of the word to which it is attached. Select the best definition for each of the words in the **ad** family. Put the number of the definition in the proper space in the Magic Square box. If the numbers going up and down and the numbers going across all add up to the same thing, you have found the magic number!

WORDS
A. adjust
B. acclaim
C. affirm
D. allocate
E. annotate
F. appointment
G. approve
H. assignment
I. attend

DEFINITIONS
1. a statement of expenses and costs
2. to praise
3. to be present and listen
4. to put into a specific place
5. to judge and find acceptable
6. to explain with notes
7. to state positively or to declare as fact
8. a time set to meet
9. to cause something to fit or be right
10. work given to be completed

Magic Square Box

A.	B.	C.
D.	E.	F.
G.	H.	I.

Magic Number _____

Copyright Dynamic Literacy LLC

www.dynamicliteracy.com

Name _____

WORD SEARCH

Words with the prefix ad- or one of its assimilated forms meaning "to or toward"

Find the words in the grid. Words can go across or up and down, straight or diagonally, forwards or backwards.

```
X J V F K A R R A N G E Y N A
W N A S S I G N M E N T M A T
K T T N O R F F A G B V T N T
Q N C X M D L H T N N T K K A
X E J A S S O R T N E M Y E C
L M A C C L A I M N I R V A H
P T T N D T M W D A Q O L J E
A N N I T G B A T F R L P W S
F I E O P X K T C P O R F P F
F O R J N K S X P C O N E X A
I P A D B U I A A J O D X S T
R P P A J F B T J M R U A K T
M A P D F R E E T A T O N N A
Z R A A T P C D G Y R D N T L
A C C O U N T A N T V Z L M M
```

acclaim	affix	approve
account	affront	arrange
accountant	allocate	arrest
adjoin	annotate	assignment
adjust	apparent	assort
adopt	appoint	attaches
affirm	appointment	attend

205

Name _____

Go For It!

Fill in the blanks using the words at the bottom of the page that all mean "to or toward something"

Why do they mean <u>to or toward something</u>? _____

1. All the money that Scrooge had managed to _____ was useless.

2. The biology class will _____ a name tag to each tree in the school yard.

3. Frieda will _____ most of her allowance to paying for her cell-phone.

4. Whom will the president _____ to take charge of the hurricane disaster?

5. The unhappy girl was required to _____ a pile of seeds into groups.

6. The guards that _____ the Queen may not smile or look at people.

7. The new band was met with great _____ when it came to town.

8. The King did not realize how it would _____ colonists to pay for tea.

9. The choir director had us _____ the sides of the sheet music with instructions.

10. George and Janet will _____ the transportation to and from their house.

<u>Check off these words as you use them.</u>

| acclaim | affix | aggrieve | allocate | amass |
| annotate | appoint | arrange | assort | attend |

PREFIX SQUARE

_____
Name

for **in-** meaning "not"

The prefix **in** (not) is also sometimes spelled **il**, **im**, or **ir**, depending on the first letter of the word to which it is attached. Start in the middle square with the prefix **in** (or one of its assimilated forms) and combine this part with the words in the other squares to build new words. Write each word and a definition you can think of for it in the spaces provided at the bottom of the page. Use the back of the page if you need to.

mature	formal	regular
mortal	il-, im-, in-, ir-	complete
literate	visible	legal

_____
_____
_____
_____
_____

Copyright Dynamic Literacy LLC   www.dynamicliteracy.com

AFFIX ADDER

_____
Name

> This prefix **in-** means "not," spelled **il**, **in**, **im**, or **ir**, depending on the first letter of the word to which it is attached.

> 1. Write **in** or one of its alternative spellings in the blank space in front of each word listed below and make a new word.
> 2. Tell what you think the new word means.
> 3. Write a sentence using the new word.

We've done one for you:

   PATIENT means able to wait

   ...so IMPATIENT means <u>not able to wait.</u>

Note that **im** is the preferred spelling of **in** because it is easier to pronounce when it attaches to the first letter of "patient."

Sentence: <u>The children were impatient for vacation to begin.</u>

---

1. LEGIBLE means easily readable

   ...so ____LEGIBLE means _____

Used in a sentence:

2. CONVENIENT means suitable

   ...so ____CONVENIENT means _____

Used in a sentence:

3. POSSIBLE means capable of happening

   ...so ____POSSIBLE means _____

Used in a sentence:

4. MOBILE means capable of moving

   ...so ____MOBILE means _____

Used in a sentence:

5. LIBERAL means free of restrictions
   ...so ____LIBERAL means _____
Used in a sentence:

6. FINITE means limited in space or time
   ...so ____FINITE means _____
Used in a sentence:

7. LOGICAL means reasonable
   ...so ____LOGICAL means _____
Used in a sentence:

8. LEGITIMATE means within the law
   ...so ____LEGITIMATE means _____
Used in a sentence:

9. DISPENSABLE means able to be thrown away or trashed
   ...so ____DISPENSABLE means _____
Used in a sentence:

10. CREDIBLE means believable
    ...so ____CREDIBLE means _____
Used in a sentence:

MAGIC SQUARE

_____
Name

for **in**- meaning "not"

The prefix **in** (not) is also sometimes spelled **il**, **im**, or **ir**, depending on the first letter of the word to which it is attached. Select the best definition for each of the words in the **in** family. Put the number of the definition in the proper space in the Magic Square box. If the numbers going up and down and the numbers going across all add up to the same thing, you have found the magic number!

WORDS
A. illegible
B. irresponsible
C. irregular
D. immature
E. insane
F. illegal
G. illiterate
H. innumerable
I. independent

DEFINITIONS
1. not attractive
2. not within expected form
3. not able to be counted
4. not adult
5. not able to read
6. not lawful
7. not able to be relied on
8. not of right mind
9. cannot be read
10. not needing support

Magic Square Box

A.	B.	C.
D.	E.	F.
G.	H.	I.

Magic Number _____

Copyright Dynamic Literacy LLC   www.dynamicliteracy.com

Name _____

WORD SEARCH

Words with the prefix in- or one of its assimilated forms meaning "not"

Find and circle all the words in the grid. Words can go across or up and down, straight or diagonally, forwards or backwards

```
T B N R H Y P N T B N V M K L Y K C L G
R D I N D I S P E N S A B L E E W A L L
W K Q C R K T W P Q H P M F L V M M T E
I I L L E G I T I M A T E B I R G J L M
N N N R K X H J Z K M G I N O W I B L Q
N D S K L V T B N M L G C F J M O K M Q
U C W A D I H N M K E R N B M N J R P W
M T X I N K N T J L E I C A G I P D L W
E D E T L E W V L D B G T I T L H Z A I
R K N T X L R I I M N U M B N L K V G N
A T N Z I P I B D S R M G W E O Y K E C
B N H K X N L T G E I L R M R G K J L O
L E K K Y E I A E M V B V H E I R L L N
E I L V X N B F T R B K L K F C M L I V
L T M J T Z V Z N R A M T E F A T L M E
J A L L R L R N R I O T J K I L J M V N
L P Z E L I B O M M I M E K D X R C T I
M M I R R E G U L A R F M M N R T R F E
M I M P V L Y D D L K G K I I W Y K D N
W N V M T T N E D N E P E D N I Q Y M T
```

ignoble	immobile	indispensable
illegal	immortal	infinite
illegible	impatient	informal
illegitimate	inconvenient	innumerable
illiterate	incredible	insane
illogical	independent	invisible
immature	indifferent	irregular

Name _____

Not!

Fill in the blanks using the words at the bottom of the page that all mean "not something."

Why do they mean <u>not something</u>? _____

1. When giving directions, don't confuse your listener with useless, _____ details.

2. Sheri spilled ink on her assignment and now the work is _____.

3. The poor _____ children that we rescued could not write their names and had never read a book.

4. Some thought that it would be _____ to reach China by sailing west.

5. Instead of paying all his bills on the first of the month, Mr. Bligh makes unpredictable, _____ payments.

6. People found it _____ that Phileas Fogg went all the way around the world in 80 days.

7. There is a law in some states that makes it _____ to bring a cow onto a school bus.

8. No one was amused by the new kid's _____ behavior and childish jokes.

9. Hoping the bees would not notice him, Scott stood _____ and silent.

10. The _____ guards accidentally let the prisoner get away.

<u>Check off these words as you use them</u>.

| illegal | illegible | illiterate | immature | immobile |

| impossible | incredible | irresponsible | irrelevant | irregular |

Copyright Dynamic Literacy LLC   www.dynamicliteracy.com

PREFIX SQUARE

_____
Name

for **in-** meaning "in, into"

The prefix **in** (in, into) is also sometimes spelled **en**, **em**, or **im**, depending on the first letter of the word to which it is attached. Start in the middle square with the prefix **in-** (or one of its assimilated forms) and combine this part with the words in the other squares to build new words. Write each word and a definition you can think of for it in the spaces provided at the bottom of the page. Use the back of the page if you need to.

tangle	power	dent
migrate	en-, em-, im-, in-	vision
port	prison	danger

_____
_____
_____
_____

Copyright Dynamic Literacy LLC   www.dynamicliteracy.com

AFFIX ADDER

_____
Name

> This prefix **in-** means "in, into," spelled **en, em, in,** or **im,** depending on the first letter of the word to which it is attached.
>
> 1. Write **in** or one of its alternative spellings in the blank space in front of each word listed below and make a new word.
> 2. Tell what you think the new word means.
> 3. Write a sentence using the new word.

We've done one for you:

FOLD means able to bend over or double up

...so EN FOLD means *to double up inside or to surround*.

Note that **en** is the preferred spelling of **in** because it is easier to pronounce when it attaches to the first letter of "fold."

Sentence: *The mother held her child closely as if to enfold him protectively.*

1. POWER means strength or might
   ...so ____POWER means _____
   Used in a sentence:

2. TANGLE means a jumbled or messy condition
   ...so ____TANGLE means _____
   Used in a sentence:

3. MIGRATE means to move and settle
   ...so ____MIGRATE means _____
   Used in a sentence:

4. DENT means a tooth-shaped mark or depression
   ...so ____DENT means _____
   Used in a sentence:

Copyright Dynamic Literacy LLC   www.dynamicliteracy.com

5. CODE means organized symbols for communication
   ...so ____CODE means _____
Used in a sentence:

6. PRISON means penitentiary or jail
   ...so ____PRISON means _____
Used in a sentence:

7. DUCT means a passageway or entrance to
   ...so ____DUCT means _____
Used in a sentence:

8. MESH means a net or screen
   ...so ____MESH means _____
Used in a sentence:

9. TRAP means to catch or ensnare
   ...so ____TRAP means _____
Used in a sentence:

10. BODY means the physical structure of a thing
    ...so ____BODY means _____
Used in a sentence:

MAGIC SQUARE

_____
Name

for **in**- meaning "in, into"

The prefix **in** (in) is also sometimes spelled **en**, **em**, or **im**, depending on the first letter of the word to which it is attached. Select the best definition for each of the words in the **in** family. Put the number of the definition in the proper space in the Magic Square box. If the numbers going up and down and the numbers going across all add up to the same thing, you have found the magic number!

WORDS
A. encase
B. encircle
C. impassion
D. inbuilt
E. imprint
F. indwell
G. emblaze
H. import
I. enrich

DEFINITIONS
1. to carry in
2. constructed in
3. to fill with feeling
4. to be located or live within something
5. to go around
6. to cause to burst into flames
7. to put in a box
8. to give a lot of money or strength to
9. to produce a mark upon by pressure

Magic Square Box

A.	B.	C.
D.	E.	F.
G.	H.	I.

Magic Number _____

Copyright Dynamic Literacy LLC   www.dynamicliteracy.com

WORD SEARCH

Words with the prefix in- or one of its assimilated forms meaning "in, into"

Find and circle all the words in the grid. Words can go across or up and down, straight or diagonally, forwards or backwards.

```
D G R G Y M L E M B A L M G E
T T E E Y D M Y E E D O C N E
N J N E N K O N L E C L J N N
E K W G K R I B L R N O F G L
N B R A V W I C M F Y O Y I W
V T A C T Q R C H E L T R M D
I K P N W I N S H D W R E P J
S E E C P E P R Z D O W R P
I M N N L M W L L R H P O E G
O M E O N T I P W N B M P S Z
N F P E R N T C U D N I M S R
K N Y E D H M F Z T N N E C N
L N K E R M T E N T A N G L E
L J N P R I W N F L U G N E D
K T T Z M R L L E H T X N M L
```

embalm	engulf	envision
embody	enjoy	enwrap
empower	enmesh	imperil
encage	enrich	import
encircle	entangle	impress
encode	enthrone	indent
enfold	entwine	induct

Are you into it?

Name _____

Fill in the blanks using the words at the bottom of the page that all mean "in or into something."

Why do they mean <u>in or into something</u>? _____

1. Being afraid of bullies serves to _____ bullies.

2. Arnie wanted to _____ the name of his favorite cause on all his shirts.

3. From what country do we _____ the most bananas?

4. My neighbors had books cases _____ in all the rooms of their new house.

5. Watch out so that you do not _____ your shoelaces in the escalator.

6. Which book has left the greatest _____ on your mind?

7. The company wants to use the wood in the forest but not to _____ the animals that live there.

8. How many people from Canada _____ to the U.S. annually?

9. With their good nature and concern for others, Frank and Frances _____ the principles of respect and humanity.

10. Can you _____ the time when there were no phones, televisions, or cars?

<u>Check off these words as you use them</u>.

| emblaze | embody | empower | endanger | entangle |
| envision | immigrate | import | imprint | inbuilt |

NOTES

NOTES